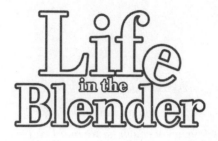

ALSO BY SANDI PATTY:

Broken on the Back Row:
A Journey through Grace and Forgiveness

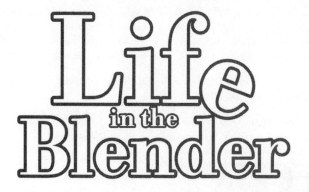

Life in the Blender

Blending Families, Lives,
and Relationships with Grace

SANDI PATTY

W Publishing Group
A Division of Thomas Nelson Publishers
Since 1798

www.wpublishinggroup.com

Published by W Publishing Group, a division of Thomas Nelson, Inc., P.O. Box 141000, Nashville, TN, 37214.

W Publishing Group books may be purchased in bulk for educational, business, fundraising, or sales promotional use. For information, please e-mail SpecialMarkets@ThomasNelson.com.

Unless otherwise indicated, Scripture quotations used in this book are from The Holy Bible, New International Version (NIV). Copyright © 1973, 1978, 1984, International Bible Society. Used by permission of Zondervan.

Other Scripture quotations are from *The Message* (MSG), copyright © 1993, 1994, 1995, 1996, 2000, 2001, 2002. Used by permission of NavPress Publishing Group. The Holy Bible, New Living Translation (NLT), copyright © 1996 by Tyndale Charitable Trust. Used by permission of Tyndale House Publishers, Wheaton, IL.

Library of Congress Cataloging-in-Publication Data

Patty, Sandi, 1956-
  Life in the blender : blending families, lives, and relationships with grace / Sandi Patty.
    p. cm.
  ISBN 0-8499-0046-8
  1. Mothers--Religious life. 2. Adoptive parents--Religious life. 3. Stepfamilies--Religious life. I. Title.
  BV4529.18.P38 2006
  248.4--dc22

2005035030

Printed in the United States of America

06 07 08 09 10 QW 9 8 7 6 5 4 3 2 1

For more information about Sandi Patty, go to www.sandipatty.com. For bookings, contact William Morris Agency, 1600 Division Street, Suite 300, Nashville, TN 37203, 615-963-3000. For management information, contact Mike Atkins Entertainment, 615-345-4554.

To my family,
   with love and thanks.
You fill this wild ride
through life with chaotic joy.

Contents

Surprises in the Rearview Mirror

I was enjoying a bit of precious mother-daughter time late one night with my then-fifteen-year-old daughter, just the two of us, without any of the other eight members of our rambunctious tribe around. Erin is a sweet girl with a big heart, and that day she was concerned about one of her friends.

"I just don't think she's telling me everything, Mom," Erin said. "It feels like she's holding something back."

"What kind of things?" I asked.

"I don't know. It's just a feeling I have," she said, a worried look on her face. "I just don't think she's telling me what's really going on."

"Well, honey, maybe that's best. Maybe there are things that, frankly, are none of your business. Maybe you don't need to know *everything*," I answered.

"But that's just it, Mom," she insisted. "I *do* need to know everything. I always want to know everything. That's just

1

the way I am. I get so worked up if I think someone's holding something back from me."

"That's interesting, sugar. Why do you think you're like that? Where did that come from?" I asked.

There was just the slightest pause as Erin looked down at her hands, probably wondering if she could tell me the truth without hurting my feelings.

"Well . . . you know . . . when I was little . . . I never felt like I knew everything about what was going on with you and Don . . ."

✳ ✳ ✳

I've wanted to write this book for years. It's estimated that more than 50 percent of the people sitting in the pews at church every Sunday have been through divorce, and many of them have moved on to a second marriage and a household that's right out of the movie *Yours, Mine, and Ours*. For more than ten years, I've been one of them.

There are so many of us, yet there's so little out there in the marketplace to help, encourage, and support us Christians in blended families.

Maybe it's because divorce has been swept under the rug by too many churches. Or maybe it's because as Christians we're expected to hold to a higher standard than the rest of the world—and the rest of the world seems to have gone divorce crazy in the last few decades.

Whatever the reason for the church's inattention, there are millions of us divorced and remarried Christians out there, sitting in the pews. Many of us are struggling through some very difficult issues, and often we're heading into uncharted territory. We need help. We need churches that will acknowledge our presence, organize support for us, and help us find those within the congregation who have been through the trials we're experiencing and who can come alongside us and offer help and encouragement. Those of us who are living in blended families need some special love and attention because we're not only coping with our own whirlwind of emotions and needs, we're trying to help our children and stepchildren survive that ride through the blender too.

That's why I've wanted to write this book, to share what I've learned and to help others who may have less experience than I do in the chop and mix cycles, whether they've ended up in a blended family through divorce or through the devastating death of a spouse.

I've wanted to write this book—and yet, this is not the book I thought I would write. In my head, I penned a pleasant little humor-sprinkled volume that told how, after a painful divorce, my four kids and I blended into one big, happy family with Don Peslis and his three kids after they too went through a difficult marital breakup. I thought I would write that there were plenty of hard times in the beginning, but we've moved on now, so that, more than ten years into this second marriage, we've all reached a pain-free place of wholesome happiness and harmony.

Actually, that's all pretty much true. But then I started thinking about those interior chapters of the book, where I would describe the prayerful, deliberate, well-thought-out steps Don and I took to get our blended family to this place of happiness and harmony—and that's when my original plans got blown out of the water. Because that's when I asked our kids for *their* perspective on what it's been like to blend our two families into one.

What our children told Don and me came as such a surprise, we stumbled away from those book-talk sessions looking like goggle-eyed cartoon characters who had just been bonked by the big sledgehammer in a carnival sideshow.

"I can't believe it," I would say to Don, nearly speechless after one of these sessions.

"Me either," he would answer, shaking his head and sharing my shock.

Priceless Moments

What a revelation! Don's and my perspective on how the blending occurred is almost totally different from the perspectives of our eight children including our adopted son, Sam, who this year will be 22, 18, 18, 18, 17, 16, 14, and 10. Yet somehow, despite the vastly different ways that process unfolded for the kids and for Don and me, we managed to achieve what we *all* had hoped and prayed for—a two-in-one family whose members love and respect each other and who now enjoy a rich, fulfilling life together.

Don's and my perspective on how the blending occurred is almost totally different from the perspectives of our eight children.

Thank goodness I asked for the kids' reflections! Our discussions about our life in the blender have given all of us greater insights into each other's thinking, and I'm happy to share those perspectives with you so that you can have more ideas about what might work best in your blended family. I believe our kids understand now that Don and I were truly doing the best we knew to do to help them through the blending process. In our discussions, we've been able to lay out for them the reasons behind our decisions and the goals that motivated our actions. And from their comments we've learned how the process felt for them—and also how we could have done things differently and better.

Best of all, those frank and honest talks have opened up a whole new avenue of communication with our children. Although we've always enjoyed a very close relationship with them and felt we had talked openly with each of our kids, it turns out we weren't talking enough—especially about the divorce and the second marriage and how they affected all of us. As they offered up their insights for this book, I was grateful they felt free to openly discuss what they went through and how our decisions influenced them. They've helped us see how our actions—and especially my own poor choices more than a decade ago—still affect them today.

Erin's comment to me that night was one of those painful but priceless moments when we took a quick trip down that new avenue of communication. She was just a toddler when her dad and I separated, and she was only six when Don and I married. Who would have thought, all these years later, that she would be able to link a specific, unfulfilled need within her life today to an unexpressed sense of insecurity she'd felt all those years ago as such a young child? And honestly, who could have known she would feel that insecurity, given all the love, hard work, and talking we did with the kids, and all the attention we paid to their physical and emotional needs as we were going through the blending process?

It did hurt to hear her admit the longing she'd been carrying with her, a longing to know she could trust that the adults in control of her life would tell her the truth, the whole truth, and nothing but the truth. And yet I am so thankful she feels safe enough today to tell me how she feels, knowing that no matter what she says, I will listen to her and love her forever. Nothing will ever change that. And who knows? Maybe by sharing these feelings with me today, she won't need to tell them to a therapist twenty years from now.

I told her, "Erin, I appreciate the fact that you're willing to tell me how you feel deep down inside. I know how hard it is to take a risk and tell someone something that you know might hurt her feelings. I'm so sorry for how I have hurt you by the choices that I've made, and I want you to know that I will answer *anything* you want to ask me anytime. I'm not going to tell you more than you want to know, but I will answer absolutely anything."

My conversation with Erin and the sessions with our other kids have caused the attitude of this book to change. All these years, I thought I would write about what I've done and what I've learned during the last fourteen years as my children and I—and Don and his children—have crossed the minefield between ending one marriage and starting another one. Indeed, the pages ahead are full of those lessons. But what our kids have helped us learn as well is that a blended family is a *continual* work in progress.

A blended family is a continual *work in progress.*

This book isn't about how we got everything right and always knew the best thing to do. We did lots of things wrong (just ask our kids!). So, more than anything, *Life in the Blender* is about the hindsight we've gained from the things we've tried and the mistakes we've made. I hope that by sharing our different perspectives and insights as well as the lessons we've learned, we can help make your ride through the blender a little less turbulent and a lot more rewarding. As my Women of Faith friend Thelma Wells says, "Learn from others' mistakes. If you're gonna make a mistake, let it be a new mistake —something you couldn't learn any other way."

Let's face it. When you dump a bunch of stuff into a blender and push the MIX button, the process is loud, and it isn't always pretty. But the result can be pretty terrific. The same is true when a mom and a dad get married. In a second marriage, the children, who probably didn't ask for any of this, get dumped into a giant blender shaped like a house. The turbulent process of blending those two families into one can get loud and crazy, and even unpleasant. But hang in there. After more than a decade of living in this wild whirlwind, I'm here to tell you, the result can be over-the-top wonderful. Come along, and I'll show you, lumps and all, how we got here.

1.

The Chop and Mix Cycles

Mending and Blending Broken Hearts

> Now we look inside, and what we see is that anyone
> united with the Messiah gets a fresh start, is created new.
> The old life is gone; a new life burgeons! Look at it!
> —2 Corinthians 5:17 MSG

First United Methodist Church in Oklahoma City, where I was born, is more than one hundred years old. Called "First Church" by its members, it stands across the street from the national memorial marking the site where the Murrah Federal Building was bombed on April 19, 1995.

The violent explosion killed 168 people, including children. While our whole nation grieved over the tragic and senseless loss of life caused by the bombing, smaller losses were mourned as well. The blast caused such severe damage to the grand old First Church structure that the congregation was displaced for three years while its destroyed sanctuary could be rebuilt. Among the treasures lost when the front walls of the old building collapsed were First Church's beautiful old stained-glass windows.

Almost before the dust settled, volunteers and church members lovingly collected the fragile shards of glass from the heaped-up rubble of the collapsed walls. Over the next five years, they carefully put those pieces back together in totally new creations—crafts, decorative items, and mementos that became beautiful and meaningful works of art.

Today, wonderful new stained-glass windows glow on the building's reconstructed façade. One of them, in the chapel, includes a single piece of unbroken glass that miraculously survived the blast. On that unblemished piece is the face of Jesus.

The windows at First Church are especially meaningful for people like me, and for families who feel like their lives have gotten all cracked up and glued back together—who know what it's like to be broken and end up in a totally new creation. We are living out the powerful truth of the inscription on one of the windows: *The Lord takes broken pieces and by His love makes us whole.*

The First Fact of Blended Families

We laugh a lot in my family. (You know, with eight kids, you have to either laugh or cry about something just about every day, so you might as well laugh. It feels better and costs less—no tissues needed. As my kids constantly remind me, "Mom, you've just gotta find the joy.") In this book, I want to share a lot of laughter with you. But before we can get to that point, there's a somber fact we have to establish. It's the difficult cornerstone all blended families share. I call it the first fact of blended families, and sadly, it's this: *every blended family is born of loss.*

> *As my kids constantly remind me, "Mom,*
> *you've just gotta find the joy."*

Whether it's through death or divorce or an unmarried parent who was never part of the picture, a blended family comes into being because something precious was lost. And that loss brings pain.

It's the pain of brokenness, a kind of hurt I know oh, so well.

My first husband and I separated after fourteen years of marriage and divorced two years later. And just let me acknowledge right here that those of us who have been through divorce dislike it when others use the word *broken,* even though we often use it to describe ourselves. Children of single-parent or blended families hate to overhear gossipers whispering to each other, "You know, those kids come from a broken home." When a marriage ends, especially when children are involved, it's not just our *home* that's broken; it's so much more than that. It's our *heart*, and we don't like to think that our innermost feelings, our anguish and hurt, are out there for public review and commentary.

A friend of mine married a wonderful man whose wife had died, and I've watched her go through many of the same issues with her stepchildren that I've experienced. No matter how you end up in a blended family, there is loss, there is pain, and it's always a challenge to *be* a parent to stepchildren without coming across as trying to *replace* the original parent.

My own blended family is the result of two divorces—Don's and mine. While it's tremendously hard on any adults and children to go through a marital breakup, in my case, I made the bad situation exponentially more painful by the poor choices I made during that already distressful time. The full story of my sin and restoration as a "new creation" in God's kingdom is told in my book *Broken on the Back Row*. But I hope this greatly condensed version will help you understand how I caused myself and my family incredible pain even beyond the "normal" agony a family goes through when it's split by divorce.

Let me just take a breath here before I lay it out for you in one succinctly sordid sentence: while I was still married to my first husband, I had an inappropriate relationship with Don Peslis, who was also married.

What I did would be a scandalous sin for anyone to commit, but frankly, I wasn't an anonymous "anyone." I traveled the world as a well-known Christian recording artist, singing out the gospel message before large audiences. But as my career peaked, my private life plummeted. Unhappy in my marriage, I found friendship, comfort, and love in another man—Don—then I lied about what was going on.

I understand and probably deserved every hurtful thing that happened to me when my shameful behavior was finally revealed and I acknowledged what I had done. Emotional upheaval, estrangement from friends and colleagues, and a career that dropped from the mountaintop to the valley seemingly overnight—those were just a few of the consequences.

I had no one but myself to blame. Still, I was determined to face my failures head-on and make a new start. I could take whatever came my way. What nearly killed me, however, was that my children got hurt by the public humiliation that descended on me, and they hadn't done *anything* to deserve it and were too young to even understand why it was happening.

Ironically, the turning point came for me one Sunday before things came to a head—while I was still in the midst of the emotional train wreck, separated from my husband and in love with Don. At that stage in my life, I felt very far from God, and I was miserable, knowing the dark secret I was living and fearing how it would affect my career and my future if it got out.

It was my turn to have the kids that weekend, and I decided to take them to a different church in our Indiana hometown. After quietly dropping the kids off in the Sunday school that morning, I settled into a seat on the back row of the balcony and cried my way through the service, quietly releasing all those pent-up emotions. When the sermon ended, the pastor stepped down from the pulpit and took a few steps down the aisle, inviting visitors to stand and introduce themselves. No way was I doing that! I didn't want anyone to know I was there.

Then that pastor, Jim Lyon, said something that took my breath away. "Maybe you've been visiting with us here this morning, and you're not ready to tell anyone your name," he said in his kind, warm voice. "Maybe all you want to do is sit on the back row of the balcony and cry. That's OK. We want you to know that the God we serve knows how to find you there. He hasn't forgotten about you. We serve the God of second chances, the God of new beginnings. We serve the God who sets His children free."

"We serve the God of second chances, the God of new beginnings. We serve the God who sets His children free."

Pastor Lyon told me later he hadn't noticed me in the congregation—didn't know that someone actually *was* sitting on the back row of the balcony, crying. But, looking back on that day, I see him in my mind's eye as someone who was walking through the rubble that day, helping me pick up the shattered pieces of my life, just as those First Church members had picked up the broken shards of their beautiful, shattered windows in Oklahoma City.

Over the next few years, he and other leaders at the North Anderson Church of God would guide me through a long and challenging process that restored me to the church and deepened my personal relationship with the One who had died so that I could be forgiven for all my sins, no matter how scandalous they were. With the help of those caring, devoted church friends, I laid those broken pieces of my life in the hands of our Savior, who "by His love makes us whole."

Pop-up Pain: Acknowledging the Hurt That Hides

All of that turmoil and grief happened so long ago, and our family is so happy and content today, that I guess I had hoped all the hard stuff had finally been put to rest and we had moved on. Maybe I actually believed we were past the hurt. That's how I first intended to write this book. But what I've learned (again) as I've collected my thoughts, along with the kids' perspectives, is that a blended family's pain doesn't necessarily end even when everything seems settled and time has faded the hardest memories. The pain may lie dormant for a while, but it's still there, and it tends to pop up occasionally, needing to be acknowledged so it doesn't fester into an even greater wound.

> *A blended family's pain doesn't necessarily end even when everything seems settled and time has faded the hardest memories.*

For me, it reappears out of the blue, as it did that day when my teenaged Erin, remembering the troubling times of divorce and remarriage during her earliest preschool days, told me she'd never felt she knew the whole truth about what was going on with the adults in her life—adults whose truthfulness she needed to trust.

Or it comes out in a simple question, as it did one night while I was watching TV with our adopted son, Sam, who settled in with me to watch a movie. Even though it was a family flick, it touched briefly on an adult theme.

"That person is married to someone else, isn't he?" nine-year-old Sam commented thoughtfully as the plot unfolded.

"Yes, he is," I said.

Sam was quiet for a moment, thinking. Then he said, "Is that what *you* did?"

"Yeah," I answered grimly. "It was."

It was just a passing moment, a fifteen-second exchange between a mother and a son, but it was also a brief episode of pop-up pain that reminded me yet again that, although it may occur in different ways and varying intensities, every blended family has to repeatedly work through the pain of brokenness to get to the beauty of wholeness.

Sometimes the pain comes in haunting images that reappear unexpectedly in my mind like bubbles rising to the surface from a ship that sank long ago. One of those images comes from the evening when my first husband and I gathered our four young children, then ages two and seven with four-year-old twins in between, and broke the news to them that Mommy and Daddy were separating, and we would no longer be living in the same house. Erin was too young (we thought) to understand what was happening, and Anna, the oldest, had already been told, one-on-one. That left the twins, Jonathan and Jennifer, to absorb the full impact of this news that would turn their world upside down.

None of the kids said a word as we explained, as gently as we could, what was going to happen. But Jenni's little face took on the saddest expression, and a single tear rolled slowly down her soft cheek. It is that tear, silently staining her precious little face, that returns to my mind again and again, reminding me of the pain our children went through.

For Don's son, Donnie, the painful image is of him as a tiny boy, crying and clinging to his daddy's leg as his parents were separating.

You don't have to be in a blended family to be haunted by these hurt-filled scenes. Recently, my Women of Faith friend Sheila Walsh described in her weekly newsletter an encounter she'd had years earlier that had left a lasting image in her mind:

I was waiting to board a flight from Dallas to Pittsburgh when I became aware of a little boy sitting beside a man I took to be his father. The boy had the airline's "unaccompanied minor" packet around his neck, so I knew he was flying alone. When it was time for children to board, the boy stood up and put his Barney backpack on. His dad walked with him to the door and bent down to hug him good-bye. When I got on the plane I realized that the child was sitting just across the aisle from me. He had his head down and his seatbelt tightly fastened. Later when we were served drinks, I noticed that he couldn't get his bag of nuts open, so I asked him if I could help. He handed me the packet. "That was my dad," he said. "I see him every summer."

"Did you have a good time?" I asked.

"Yes," he replied. Then he turned his face away, toward the window, and said, "I'm not crying."

My heart ached for that little boy. He was only about six years old and already his life was torn in two and his heart was broken. I wondered if he carried the burden of blaming himself for his parents' separation, as so many children from divorced families do.

It was so like Sheila to reach out to that little boy with kindness—and also with prayer. Her story shows us something good that can come from this hurt that doesn't go away, these pieces of pop-up pain that remind us where we've been. By remembering our own time of brokenness, we can offer Christ's love and comfort to others whose lives still lie in pieces amid the rubble. We can show them through our actions—and when it's appropriate, through our words—what Sheila wrote in her newsletter: "There is healing in the will of God, a pulling together of all the pieces of our lives. It doesn't mean that we will always understand what is happening to us, but we bring our torn edges to him who holds us together."

Loss of Place

Besides the loss of an intact family of origin, those living out life in the blender face other losses as well. Many times the children will lose their birth-order rank. For example, Donnie was the oldest of Don's three kids, so he enjoyed the status of being big brother to two little sisters, of being the "little man" who shared a special place in the family lineup. That ended when Don and I married. In our blended family, Donnie landed smack-dab in the middle of the birth-order rankings. He went from having all the status and privilege of being the firstborn (at least as much status and privilege as one can manage when he's four years old) to becoming that socially disparaged cliché: the middle child.

Donnie admits now that it was a little rough, but although he gave up his oldest-child ranking, he quickly established his undisputed place as the family comedian; we can always count on him to crack a joke or make some comment that causes the room to erupt in laughter. Donnie also wants me to tell you that, although he is not the oldest child in our blended family, he is "still the coolest."

> *Adults and children in blended families may lose a*
> *literal sense of place—their family home.*

In addition, adults and children in blended families may lose a literal sense of place—their family home. The transition phases that they bump over as they go from intact family through separation, divorce, possible relocation to another city or state, remarriage, and blending can take a toll on children—and their parents too. They may find themselves living in a different place at each different phase, maybe having to change schools and make new friends while missing their old ones. Sometimes changing financial situations mean the children leave a house where everyone had his or her own room and move into cramped temporary (or permanent) quarters.

Early during my separation from their dad, my four kids and I crowded into my parents' smaller home when it was my turn to have them with me. Before Don moved into a bigger home after his divorce, he temporarily lived in a one-bedroom apartment where Donnie and his two little sisters would sleep crossways on Don's bed while he slept on the couch when it was their turn to be with their dad.

One of our kids remembers that during the transition "sometimes we bought milk on a certain day when the coupon was good, and there were times when we couldn't have cereal for breakfast because there was no milk. We went from having huge meals every night—salad, meat, two vegetables, and dessert every night—to having simple suppers, like sandwiches or a bowl of soup."

Find the Joy!

Thinking about those days, our hearts ache to think how confusing and exhausting life must have been for our weary kids as they were passed back and forth between parents and houses and, in my kids' case, lived in different homes on various days of the week, every week. It was a hard time.

Yet there's something surprising in those challenging memories too: laughter. As Don says, "Some of our best memories came from those days when Donnie, Aly, Mollie, and I were becoming a new family, just the four of us, in the apartment and later in the two-bedroom house. We got to know each other all over again; we got to know who we really are."

They still laugh about some funny things that happened as they were settling into their new life as a different kind of family. Some of those stories are about Aly's and Donnie's various sleepwalking and sleep-talking adventures. The three children, all under age six or so, shared a single bedroom and a set of bunk beds, with Donnie sleeping on top and the two girls sleeping in the bottom bed. As Donnie tells it now, it took awhile to adjust to their new sleeping arrangements.

"We were sleeping, and I had to go to the bathroom," he said. "I climbed down the ladder. Well, for a little kid, climbing down that ladder was a pretty good distance, and our bathroom wasn't very far from our room. So in my sleep state, when I got to the bottom of the ladder, I figured I was in the bathroom, but I was actually standing right by the girls' bed. I dropped trou and . . ."

You can imagine what it was like for Don, sleeping in the other room, to be awakened in the middle of the night by the hysterical screams of his two little girls.

Now, this is something that could happen in any family, blended or not. But to Don and his kids this has become one of the little "private" memories they now laugh about and claim as a part of their family's unique history. It's something that helped the four of them establish their new identity. OK, so it's not pretty. But it sure is funny—*now*, at least.

Don and his kids enjoyed that time when it was "just them" living in the little house. He says now that it was an important step, a buffer that gave him, as a newly single parent with custody of his kids, time to help him and his kids adjust to and understand who they were as a family. And it prompts him to offer this advice to others coming out of a divorce or spousal death situation: "Don't rush into a second marriage," he says. "Don't move on to that next step until you and your kids have a good sense of who you really are."

> *Don and his children established new traditions,*
> *like Super Wind-Down on Friday evenings*

To do that, Don and his children established new traditions, like Super Wind-Down on Friday evenings, when they would push back the furniture, drag out the sleeping bags, rent some movies, pop some popcorn, play board games, and enjoy a lively living-room camp-out. Now they all remember those days as a special time when they spent more time laughing than they did missing what they had lost.

They weren't necessarily easy days—Don was a single dad with custody of the three kids, working for the YMCA in wellness and also attending college classes to finish his degree. Money was tight, space was limited, and there were many stressful days. They had to look for the joy in their new circumstances; it didn't come searching for *them*. But together, they found it.

What Matters Is the Journey

Recently I developed a new way of looking at those days after reading an essay in the *Spiritual Renewal Bible* (Tyndale, 1998) linked to the verse in Matthew that says, "But you are to be perfect, even as your Father in heaven is perfect" (5:48 NLT).

Honestly, I used to hate that verse! I couldn't think of a single instant in my life when I had been perfect, and there didn't seem to be much chance of it happening in the future. But in this essay, writer Stephen Arterburn points out that the Greek word for *perfect* is *teleios,* which means "the goal, the consummation, the final purpose toward which we are moving" and also "carries the sense of 'complete,' 'mature,' or 'being at the proper stage at the proper time.'" For example, he says, "A blossoming tree can be 'perfect' even though there is no fruit because it is at the appropriate stage for fruit to be produced in time. . . . What matters to God is the journey, not just the arrival at the goal. God's concern is not that we've arrived but that we continue to face and travel in the right direction. For his grace both empowers our obedience and forgives our failures."

Faith is a compass, not a stopwatch. If you look at life through that lens, you can accept that you're living out God's plan for yourself, even if it doesn't seem to be what the rest of the world might consider "perfect" at the time.

When Don and I got married, Pastor Jim Lyon gave us a beautiful china cup and saucer. He enclosed a letter with the gift, explaining that this is the china he and his wife, Maureen, have in their home. Maureen grew up in Seattle, and as a child she often accompanied her mother to a big downtown department store, where she admired that china displayed in one of the store's windows. She never forgot the experience and reminisced about it occasionally to her friends and family.

When he was ready to propose to her, Jim bought a cup and saucer in that beautiful pattern, put the engagement ring in the cup, and presented it to Maureen. On their wedding day, he gave her a dinner plate, and on every wedding anniversary since then, he has given her a piece of that beautiful china. They now have six complete five-piece place settings.

As a wedding gift, he had a Lenox Autumn cup and saucer shipped to us from Seattle.

Well, one weekend I came home from a performance somewhere, and the cup's handle was broken off. During one of the kids' rushing passes through the house, it had been accidentally knocked off the shelf where it was displayed.

I cried when I saw it, remembering the meaning it carried,

and the kids were crushed. We glued the handle back on as best we could, and yes, we can still see the crack. But you know what? Somehow that cup brings me more joy and seems even more meaningful to me now than it did before, maybe because it helps me remember all that our pastor did to help us put our broken lives back together. And you know what else? That cup now is the sturdiest piece of china in my house. It's had other tumbles off the shelf, and that handle is still intact. It is, indeed, stronger in the broken places.

> *Hard times can make us miserable,*
> *or they can bring out the best in us.*

The cracked cup reminds me of something else: the lesson that hard times can make us miserable, or they can bring out the best in us. Look around you, and you'll see examples of those two extremes every day: dour and bitter complainers who curse the hand life has dealt them—and outward-focused angels who always manage to find the joy and give others a hand, even amid their own hardships. You may or may not have chosen the circumstances you and your children find yourselves facing right now. But either way, you can start to make those difficult circumstances better simply by aiming your attitude toward heaven and seeking out every shred of joy you can find. Often it's found in helping others.

I don't know about you, but I am so much more encouraged by someone who is willing to share her hurts with me rather than trying to make me believe she has it all together. Aren't you glad Jesus didn't say to us, "Come to me, all you who have your act together?" I would be left out for sure! Instead He says, "Come to me, all you who are *weary* and *burdened,* and I will give you rest" (Matthew 11:28, emphasis mine). And surely that's most of us living in blended families.

In this book, I hope I can help you and your family have a smoother ride through the blender by sharing the lessons I've learned and the insights I've gained (usually the hard way). If I can help you, then we'll both find the joy in our time together as we share a whirlwind ride that takes our blended families from all-cracked-up to over-the-top.

2.

Set the Anchor

The Primary Relationship

. . . forsaking all others, be faithful unto him as long as
you both shall live.

—Traditional wedding vow

In our ten-plus years of marriage, I've discovered a lot of
wonderful and amazing things about having Don Peslis as
my husband, but one of my favorites is also one of the simplest
(and certainly the cheapest). When I'm on the road for bookings, whether I'm gone a day or a week, we talk on the phone
frequently, sometimes several times a day. So it's not like we
haven't been in touch with each other while we've been
apart. But when the trip is over, I fly back to Indianapolis and
make the one-hour drive to our home, often chatting with
Don and/or the kids by cell phone on the way, especially if
I'm arriving at a time when Don isn't at work.

On those days, I turn onto our street, and as soon as I spot our house, more times than not, Don is standing in the driveway, waiting for me, a huge smile on his face. I jump out of the car, and he wraps me in his arms and makes me feel like the queen of the universe coming home from a distant planet. Honestly, the Prize Patrol bearing a million-dollar check couldn't get a better welcome than Don gives me when I come home from a road trip.

> *He wraps me in his arms and makes me feel like the queen of the universe coming home from a distant planet.*

Now, Don isn't one to sit around watching TV or twiddling his thumbs, so he was probably in the house or out in the yard, working with one of the kids on some project as I was driving home. It would have been much more convenient for him to just look up from whatever he was doing and wave hello to me as I came in, maybe blow me a kiss and tell me to leave my luggage in the car and he'll carry it in later. But that's not what he does. When he thinks I'm getting close, he stops what he's doing, and he heads for the driveway. The best analogy I can make is that he reminds me of a big ol' puppy dog, waiting for its little girl to come home from school. I swear, if he had a tail, it would be wagging!

I greet him the same way when he's been gone a day or

more. During the summer of 2004 he was gone six long weeks, living in San Diego with his brother so he could finish up his master's degree in character education, and I missed him almost more than I could bear. The only thing that saved me was that we did manage to meet in Hawaii over the July 4 holiday when I performed a concert there.

The fact is, we're crazy about each other, and we want our kids to see us showing our love and devotion to each other. Our willingness to stop what we're doing and welcome each other home from a long trip is symbolic of the way we prioritize our family life. For ten years, we've made time for each other. On a regular basis we set other things aside and make our marriage a priority. So here it is, Sandi Patty's second fact about surviving life in the blender: *the husband and wife's relationship is primary.*

Prioritizing Our Relationship

In our first marriages, Don and I saw what happens when work and parenting responsibilities hijack a couple's time. It's so easy to let every minute of the day and night fill up with tasks that simply "have" to be done, especially when you have two careers and a houseful of children. But who makes those "have-to's" the priority? And if they weaken the relationship that stands as the foundation of the family, are those other things really priorities?

When you hear couples in successful marriages say they "have to work at" their relationship, it means they may have to work extra hard at a task or a job so they can finish it up in order to have time for their spouse later. Or it means they have to deliberately choose to set aside something that seems personally important in order to share something with their spouse that enriches their marriage. Or, when you have eight children, as Don and I do, it means you work to find trustworthy baby-sitters (we often hired two at a time) so you can slip away and spend time together, just the two of you. And once you find those baby-sitters, it may also mean you have to steel yourself against your kids' whining and crying, begging you not to go as you head out the door.

> *Resolve to not let anything minor keep you from reinforcing the major relationship in your life.*

Don't fall for it! Resolve to not let anything minor keep you from reinforcing the major relationship in your life. When the kids were hollering and carrying on, Don and I had a tongue-in-cheek motto: If there's no blood, we don't come.

In busy families like ours, evenings for the husband and wife to spend alone—Don and I call them date nights—don't just happen. They have to be scheduled. My advice is that you write those plans in ink on your calendar, tell your kids about them in advance, and don't let anything but near-death experiences or major dismemberment keep you from carrying them out. (Just kidding—malaria and hurricanes are also approved exceptions.) When the kids were little we made a habit of setting date night on one of the weekday evenings when my four children were at their dad's house. Then we just needed one sitter to watch the other four (Don's three plus our adopted Sam by that time).

Date night doesn't have to be extravagant or elaborate. Believe it or not, even now, Don and I sometimes just slip away and go to a fast-food drive-through then sit in the car to eat and talk. The key is that when we're alone together, we are *together*. We focus on each other, we hold hands, we laugh at each other's jokes (even when we've heard them before), and we say encouraging and loving words to each other. We nurture each other, and in doing so, we strengthen our relationship. We've learned that just being alone and getting to talk without a bunch of youngsters constantly popping up beside us asking questions and requiring referee services can be a wonderful thing. We've also accumulated a delightful assortment of adult friends, and we enjoy going out with them for dinner or a show or a gathering at someone's house.

I *love* going out with Don. As my kids would say, he is the *funnest* person to be with. He is warm and witty, kind and considerate, clever and creative. Sometimes I consider the road I've traveled and the mistakes I've made, and I get teary-eyed thinking how blessed I am now that I get to share the rest of my life with this man. And, not to brag, but I sorta think Don feels the same way about me.

Even though we're crazy about each other, it would be oh, so easy to let other things steal our time together. In fact, it's something we still struggle with, even though it should be much easier now that the kids are older. Someone's always all stirred up about something urgent. There's always something that needs your attention and pushes "less immediate" priorities to the sidelines. But Don and I do everything we can to let our kids see that our overall priority is our personal relationship with the Savior, and our earthly priority is the relationship we have with each other. It is the foundation on which our children can feel loved and secure.

Keeping It Fresh

Not only does it take work to make the marital relationship a priority, it also requires a little creativity. Don and I love to surprise each other with gifts and special goings-on. Last year for my birthday, he "kidnapped" me—zipped in and whisked me away before I knew what was happening and took me out for a lovely dinner and then off to a Michael Buble concert, where I felt personally serenaded by an evening of wonderfully romantic jazz, blues, and big-band music. Afterward, we even got to meet Michael Buble and have our photo taken with him.

I pulled off quite a surprise too, if I do say so myself. I wish you could have seen Don's face when he came home last year after finishing his portfolio, one of the last steps toward completing his master's degree, and found my graduation gift for him. On that particular day he was probably a little disappointed that the kids and I *weren't* standing in the driveway, waiting to congratulate him and celebrate his latest achievement. The fact was, we were all peeking out from the shrubbery and hiding behind the gate as he drove home, pulled into the driveway, and pushed the button on the visor of his huge black Suburban to open the garage door. His eyes were as big as Frisbees when he saw what was waiting in his usual parking spot: the cute little black sports car he'd admired several times as we drove by it at one of the local dealerships!

> *His eyes were as big as Frisbees when he saw what was waiting in his usual parking spot.*

To understand just how special this car is to Don, you have to remember that he is the dad in a blended family totaling *ten* people. For the last decade he's felt more like a school-bus driver than the NASCAR competitor he imagines himself to be. So now here he is, the owner of a *two-seater* roadster. Forget hauling a bunch of kids around; he can barely fit a gym bag in that thing! In fact, it's so small it came with an instruction booklet explaining how, if you carefully follow the directions, you can load a golf bag into the incredibly tiny space behind the seats. It's his baby, but he *has* let me drive it a few times. In fact, as he's quick to tell everyone, *I* am the one who got the first speeding ticket in it. With three hundred horsepower under the hood of this car the size of a sardine can, I fear there may be several more to come!

Laying the Foundation

Maybe you're thinking I sound callous when I say that the marriage relationship is primary—implying that the parent-child relationship is secondary. After all, the children have been through so much. Shouldn't *they* be the priority, the center around which everything in the blended family whirls?

Certainly our children's well-being *is* a priority. Ensuring their safety and their emotional and physical welfare is absolutely essential, especially after they've endured the turmoil of divorce or the death of a parent and have had to adjust to life in a blended family. They need to feel cherished and loved, and they need to know without a doubt that they're living in a secure and stable environment, even if that environment includes moving between two different homes.

My theory is that there's no better way to provide that stability and security than to let your children see you and your spouse showing sincere and affectionate devotion to each other. When children see their parent and stepparent loving each other and making their relationship a priority, they come to feel that their household situation will be the same tomorrow as it is today. They can go to sleep at night knowing they'll wake up in the morning and the adults who are in charge of their life will still be there, watching over them and maintaining a stable home for them. In other words, they slowly regain the trust that may have been damaged when their original parents divorced or even when one of their parents died. Knowing that the foundation of their blended family is strong, children develop confidence that helps them venture out, believing their family will still be there for them, steady and sure, when they come back home.

As an analogy, think of a toddler and his mother going to a park. The toddler finds himself in a new, unfamiliar place, and at first he clings warily to his mother, watching wide-eyed as the other children play. Then maybe he turns loose of Mom's hand for a moment and takes a couple of steps toward those laughing playmates-to-be. In an instant he's back on his mother's lap, needing that touch of security. But then he scoots down and heads out again, and soon he's happily playing with his new friends.

But as he plays, he's constantly checking in with Mom, looking for her, smiling when he sees she's still there, smiling back at him. He needs to be able to count on her, to know she's there for him, and when she proves herself to be steady and dependable, he gradually gains the trust and confidence he needs to venture out and try new things.

When Don and I got married in August 1995 in a beautiful outdoor setting in Estes Park, Colorado, our kids were an important part of the ceremony. My son Jonathan *and* my dad, Ron Patty, walked me down the aisle. Donnie stood up with Don as his best (little) man. Don and I made vows to each other's children, and as we exchanged rings with each other, we also gave each child a little ring, worn on a chain. It was engraved, "With our love, Dad and Sandi" (or "Mom and Don").

We wanted to assure our children that they would always be a big priority in our lives. But at the same time, we were letting them see that we were creating a new, higher priority that would benefit them as much as it delighted us. That priority was—and still is—our relationship with each other.

That Old Friend, Imperfection

Wouldn't it be great if, after all the good things I've said about our marriage, I could add that in our ten-plus years together Don and I have never raised our voices at each other, never lost our temper, never argued, never slammed a door, never hung up the phone in the middle of the other's sentence? Wouldn't it be great if we had a *perfect* relationship?

And while we're fantasizing, wouldn't it be great if we could eat chocolate all day and be a size 4?

> *While we're fantasizing, wouldn't it be great*
> *if we could eat chocolate all day and be a size 4?*

In so many ways, I grew up in a perfect family, reared by loving parents who worked in music and ministry all their lives. Mom and Dad gave my two brothers and me the most wonderfully stable and encouraging upbringing any child could hope for. And today, as Nana and Papa, they're nurturing their grandchildren in the same godly way.

I don't have a single memory of my parents arguing. If they ever said a harsh word to each other, it was out of my hearing. What a blessing it was to grow up in that family.

And yet . . .

My parents tell me now that they did argue occasionally. They did get irritated with each other from time to time. They didn't have a perfect marriage, but they hid its imperfections from their children, wanting to shield us from their private disputes.

As a result, I grew up without seeing how adults' normal conflict got resolved. I didn't learn how to respond

appropriately when someone I loved did or said something hurtful, whether it was accidental or intentional.
Because I never saw my parents show anger, I grew up
thinking I must be flawed somehow whenever I got mad.

I'd like to say I figured this out by myself, but most of these
revelations came during the time I spent in a residential therapy center during those dark days after my first marriage had
ended and the music world was poised to (rightfully) con-
demn me as a sinner and a hypocrite. I am so thankful for the
skilled and Scripture-guided professionals there who helped
me see that *all* our emotions—even anguish, even anger—are
gifts God gives us to deal with the pressures and pleasures of
our lives.

> *I don't worry that, although my relationship*
> *with Don is primary, it isn't perfect.*

So I don't worry that, although my relationship with
Don is primary, it isn't perfect. I don't fret when occasionally one or more of the kids catch us arguing. I don't rush
to call in a therapist when they witness one of my famous
I'm-so-mad-I've-just-got-to-CLEAN-something tizzies
(more on that in the next chapter). I want to let the kids see
that the more you love someone, the more passionate
you're going to be in all your emotions. You're going to have

conflicts, and that's OK. It doesn't mean the world is coming to an end. So sometimes Don and I argue in front of the kids, but we make sure they see us resolve the argument without bloodshed or lawyers. And I join in their laughter later when they mimic my mad-mama cleaning frenzies.

We've carefully tried to show them that our relationship can withstand imperfection and that our lives together are much richer because of our flaws. An incident that happened during an ocean cruise several years ago provided the perfect illustration of that truth. Those of you who've been on cruises know that usually the ship stops at different ports where passengers can get off the ship to shop or sightsee. Some of these stops are interesting, and some, well, it's just better to stay on board the boat, which is what I usually choose to do.

At this particular port somewhere in the Caribbean, however, I decided to get off and explore a bit. Near the dock was a cluster of shops selling jewelry, perfume, T-shirts, and souvenirs. But it was the little art shop that caught my eye. The captivating painting in the window drew me inside, and as I looked around I saw copies of that same painting from the window displayed all over the store. There must have been fifty or more of them, all depicting that same Caribbean seascape at sunset. As I looked more closely at one of the pictures, I decided it was just about as perfect as a painting could be. Enclosed in a lovely complementary frame, it was breathtaking. I was shocked that the price was so low, twenty-five dollars for a large, framed picture. I couldn't believe it. It looked so much more expensive than that.

Then, as I continued to browse, something else caught my eye. It was the same picture I had been seeing, but this one was slightly different. It was a little rougher, a little less polished; you could see a smudge here and there that the other pictures didn't have. There was no beautiful frame; it was just a stretched canvas with frayed edges, so to me it looked a little tacky compared with the other pictures that seemed so perfect.

I remember thinking, *Wow, if the others are only twenty-five dollars, this one must just cost two or three.* But to my surprise, I turned over the price tag and saw that it cost *two thousand* dollars! I couldn't believe it. I thought there must be a mistake.

"I don't understand," I told the clerk. "Those framed paintings seem perfect, yet they cost so much less than this one that seems a little rough."

She quickly and enthusiastically explained. "Oh, that's because the artist actually touched this canvas with his own hands. The others are just reproductions, and their flaws have been airbrushed out," she said. "You see, it is the flaws and the imperfections that make it authentic. It is because of those smudges and 'mistakes' that we can tell it is the real thing. It is the work of the master artist, and it is exactly how he created it."

I stood there looking at that store clerk as if she had just told me the priceless secret to contentment and peace—because she had! You never know where you're going to run into an inspiring sermon in your everyday life, do you? As my pastor dad would say, "That'll preach!"

I came away from that art shop vowing to always strive to be real and authentic, even if it means letting my flaws and imperfections show.

There are so many days when I would love to take an airbrush to the canvas of my life and fix all the mistakes in my past—and so many days when I wish Don and I could have a perfect relationship that was never marred by anger or arguing. But humans aren't perfect, and if we pretend to be, we're faking it.

Humans aren't perfect, and if we pretend to be, we're faking it.

Think of the apostle Paul, who prayed three times for the "thorn in [his] flesh, a messenger of Satan" to be taken away (2 Corinthians 12:7). We don't know what that "thorn" was, but it was obviously some blemish in Paul's physical body or emotional makeup. As he prayed and processed and wrestled with what he knew to be true, he was able to come to a place where he finally said, "OK, here is the secret of contentment that I have found. I know what it is like to be flawed, to be hungry and poor. I know what it is like to be needy and to have nothing. I even know what it is like to have stuff—good stuff in my life. But that is not what brings contentment." (I am seriously paraphrasing Philippians 4:12–13 here.) "Here it is. Here is the secret, the key to abundant life: I can do everything—*everything*—through Him who gives me the strength to do so."

I pray today that as you embrace your flaws and imperfections, you will remember and know in your deepest "knower" that God is the master artist. You have been touched by His hand, and His touch makes you authentic, flaws and all. Don't be afraid to let those smudges show.

Maybe you're like me and have things in your past you would like to erase. Maybe now you're in a blended family, and you're trying to make your relationship with your husband a strong, Christ-centered priority, but somehow you can't quite pull it off. Maybe some kind of "thorn" is distracting you; perhaps anger or arguments are discouraging you. Hang in there. And hang on to the One who gives you the strength to do His good will.

Your relationship with your husband needs to be your number-one earthly priority. But that relationship doesn't have to be perfect. Remember the ironic promise of Psalm 118:22: "The stone which the builders rejected has become the chief cornerstone" (NKJV). Maybe during your past you've felt left behind in the reject pile. Maybe life in the blender has left you cracked up and bruised. Remember that

God can find you there. He can restore you to a sound relationship with Him, and He can help you make your relationship with your spouse a priority that reassures and strengthens your blended family.

Amen and amen.

3.

Can We Talk?

Family Communication, Blender Style

Then you will know the truth, and the truth will set you
free.

—John 8:32

ere's the way I thought this chapter would unfold: I
planned to tell you all the successful and effective ways Don
and I communicated with our children as we were going
through divorce and remarriage. Maybe it was rather arro-
gant of me, but I was going to urge you to follow our excel-
lent example and talk, talk, talk to your kids about what
was happening so there would be no misunderstandings,
no repercussions later on.

You would see how creative and insightful we were in the
way we conducted family meetings to air any current issues
and to share information about what was going on. I thought

I would tell you how beneficial professional counseling had been for us as well as our children. And I would remind you that our families had known each other for years. Our children attended the same schools, and during our courtship, we had more family outings than just-us-two dates.

I would tell you that when Don and I and all the kids were together yet again for a Super-Wind-Down Friday, Anna, the oldest at nine, asked, "So, are you two going to get married?" We answered, "Yes!" The kids cheered. Don and I kissed, and we all headed into the happily ever after.

That's what I was going to write about in this chapter. That was Plan A.

Here's how I ended up with Plan B: As I was beginning to put this book together, I thought the kids might feel more comfortable talking with an objective third party about the wonderful way we had blended our two families into one. So I invited a friend to come in and help me "interview" some of the older kids about their memories and perceptions. After I laid out for her all the steps Don and I had taken to ensure that open communication was stressed, that we managed to find plenty of one-on-one time with each child, and that the kids were well prepared for life in their new blended family, my friend asked my daughter Jenni (who we also call Jenn) and Don's son, Donnie, who were both seventeen then, "So, what was it like when your two families blended into one?"

JENN: It was . . . we were kind of thrown for a loop. We

didn't know what was going on. Suddenly there were these other people living in our house that we really didn't know all that well.

DONNIE: It was weird. I'd always shared a room with my sisters, and all of a sudden I'm sharing a room with Jonathan. I guess it was better because at least I was rooming with a boy. But Jonathan and I hadn't always gotten along in school ever since that fight on the playground. [Donnie has always said the fight was because he was establishing himself as the "second-grade stud."]

JENN: And everything was so secretive while it was happening. We've found out now that it was just stupid to have all those secrets. We were thinking, *Why wouldn't you have told us that?* And I think it was especially hard for me because I've always wanted to be independent, but there were also times when I wanted help with homework or I wanted to just be able to talk to Mom, but it seemed like others always needed her attention. So I couldn't get that quality time when I could just talk to Mom one-on-one.

DONNIE: Basically all of us felt that way.

JENN: Maybe it's that way in any big family, but especially when it's a blended family, you can't help but feel that the other kids, especially the "new" kids, are getting all the attention. And also, when we were with my dad, we would be told one thing, and when we were with Mom, we would hear something different. I was constantly trying to decide which version to accept, which thing to believe.

How They Saw It: Apples and Oranges

After all the work Don and I had done to prepare the kids—all the talks we'd had and the time we'd shared with them before our marriage—we were shell-shocked to hear how *they* remembered the actual blending process. To hear them tell it, we did everything wrong!

> *To hear them tell it, we did everything wrong!*

The surprises continued in another session when the topic of family meetings was brought up. Frankly, I considered these frequent gatherings one of the cornerstones of our successful family life. I started organizing them with just my four kids after I came back from my stay at the residential therapy center, where I had learned how valuable it is for everyone in a group (or a family) to check in from time to time and make sure everyone knows what's going on and has a safe place to air any issues or grievances.

So my assessment of our family meetings is that they've always worked quite well, and Don agrees with me. On the other hand, here's how our conversation went when the kids were describing them:

ANNA: Mom or Don gets on the intercom and says, "Come down right now for a family meeting!" And immediately you hear someone say, "Oh, can I please be excused?" And then someone else says, "Me too!" and "Yeah, can I be excused too?"

OK, this is Sandi again. I just want to say in my defense that if I'm calling a family meeting that night, I usually put a note on the kitchen bulletin board that morning notifying everyone of the family meeting, and I also remind the kids as they're leaving for school.

JENN: We don't enjoy family meetings. Sometimes they're about nothing.

ANNA: And there are the individual "meetings," when you hear, "Anna, I need to see you a minute in the living room." And then they'll add, "You're not in trouble."

DONNIE: And then when they *don't* say that, you think, *Oh, boy.* I think I had the most trips to the living room of anyone.

JENN: That was the bad-news room. If they called you in there, you knew there was something bad going on.

ANNA: But a regular, all-family meeting is in the kitchen. It usually takes a long time for everyone to gather, and some of us get tired of waiting and drift back to what we were doing, so there are lots of calls on the intercom.

Mom is usually the one who has the agenda about whatever topic we're supposed to discuss. Maybe it's something like this year's family vacation—where and when we're going to go. Mom will throw out the choices or ask a question when we're all finally sitting around the kitchen table; the majority of us are doodling on the calendar she printed out for us. Of course, this may be the one time this week that we've all been together, so we're talking and joking and laughing.

Pretty soon, Mom will quietly say, "Well, if no one's going to talk about it, I'll talk to myself."

Then Don will give us a fifteen-minute lecture on how we need to respect Mom and give her our attention. As soon as Don starts talking, Donnie starts cracking jokes, and we all start laughing again. Then Don says, "You know what, Sandi? I just feel like we might as well go upstairs and talk to ourselves, because no one here is listening."

So maybe Don leaves. Then the cleaning begins. Mom starts cleaning, and she cleans very forcefully so we can all hear the cleaning happening. She's loading the dishwasher or emptying the dishwasher and rattling those dishes and slamming those cabinet doors. Then she starts wiping the counters like she's going to scrub the tops right off of them.

✳ ✳ ✳

I have to admit that I laughed along with everyone else as the kids were reliving what it's like in our family meetings. And I also have to admit that when something irritates me, I start cleaning. I tend to wear my feelings on my sleeve, and I also try to think of every possible ramification of a decision before it's made. But since nobody can do that, invariably I miss something. And I just hate that.

Let's say I've called a family meeting to discuss possible vacation places and dates, and someone will say, "I don't know . . . none of those times really work for me. I thought you knew I had yada-yada-yada then, Mom."

Then I'll get really quiet, devastated that I hadn't remembered that potential scheduling conflict. Everyone else is moving on to other topics, the vacation plan is out the window, and I'm taking it all very personally. That's when I start cleaning.

I know it's strange, but it's the way I am. Just sharing my testimony, as my friend Chonda Pierce would say.

Claiming they "didn't know what was going on" and ridiculing our family meetings weren't the only things the kids complained about as they evaluated the family-merging procedures we set up. They ridiculed the counseling sessions we sent them to as well. Keep in mind that ours wasn't a private, off-the-radar-screen scandal, divorce, and remarriage. The whole thing, every chapter, was played out in the national press. We thought—we *knew*—that the kids couldn't help but hear disturbing gossip and harsh remarks about our situation, and we wanted to make sure they had the professional help they needed to work through that troubling time.

JENN: We were forced to go to the counselor. Maybe in the end it was good, but we just hated it.

DONNIE: No one ever paid so much money just to play board games. All we did was play *Happy Days*.

ANNA: If I were giving advice, I'd say, don't assume your

kids need to go to counseling. We were so young, and we had to go to counseling before we knew everything that had happened, so it seemed we were going for no reason.

We thought, Why are we in counseling? What did Dad and Sandi do? It must have been bad, or else they wouldn't send us here.

DONNIE: We thought, *Why are we in counseling? What did Dad and Sandi do? It must have been bad, or else they wouldn't send us here.* It would have been better if you had just talked to us and told us what was happening. I was one who never talked about my feelings, never opened up about what the divorce was like for me. I'm the kind of kid who holds everything inside until it makes me really sick. Remember, Sandi, I ended up spending a night in the hospital in the middle of all of it.

Selective Memory, Accomplished Goals

I do remember that difficult time and how Donnie's little body just seemed to shut down because of all his pent-up emotions. But that incident just pushed us to try harder to do all the things we thought we should do to help ease our kids' passage through the grind of the blender.

"I'm in shock," I told them. "We tried so hard. We wanted to do the best we possibly could to help you through all the hard parts."

For a while, I felt flattened by what our children had said, even though they had woven humor through their comments and kept us laughing during every session. But then some reassuring thoughts sneaked into my head.

The first one came from the friend who had helped start the interview process with the kids. "Sandi, no matter what they say, look at how things turned out. Everything you and Don hoped for, prayed for, and worked for has come about. You have a strong, unified, devoted family that's obviously full of love for each other."

She told me about a similar experience with her own kids. She and her husband's career had involved lots of travel, and she said, "We just about killed ourselves working out a schedule so that one of us was *always* home with the kids." Then one day she overheard her teenage daughter telling a friend, "My parents were never home. My brother and I basically raised ourselves."

Oh, the hurts and headaches we parents must endure!

At work, Don mentioned what had happened to his boss, an educator. She told him, "Kids have selective memory. We all do. Don't dwell on what they're saying. Just look at how things have turned out. You have a wonderful family, and it's because of the way you and Sandi worked to make it that way."

Then the same kind of thought popped up in my own head as I considered how Don and I had sat there and listened to the kids lay out everything we had done wrong. It was an image that brought a smile to my face and reassurance to my heart: *our relationship with our children is strong enough for them to feel safe in telling us what we've done "wrong," knowing we'll listen to them and love them always, no matter what.*

When it all came together in my head, I had to call Don. "You know, we must have done *some* things right," I said, "or else our family wouldn't be so great today."

"You're right," he said. "We did just fine."

So. Back to Plan A and a quick review of some of the things we absolutely did right that fostered the strong and supportive (albeit occasionally funny and sarcastic) communication we enjoy today in our blended family. And yes, some things we did wrong too.

Family Meetings Revisited

I would just like to clarify that, even though the kids don't seem to remember any of them, there *have* been family meetings when we actually accomplished something. It's the only practical way to plan that all-important summer vacation or lay out our expectations about homework and grades to all the kids or ask how everyone feels about inviting a guest into our home for an extended stay.

The "meetings" grew out of a practice I started with my four kids when we were on our own. At supper each evening, to help foster conversation, we would go around the dinner table, taking turns describing the highs and lows of our day. Or maybe I would ask, "On a scale of one to ten, how was your day?" and ask each child to elaborate on that rating.

I've tried every way I can to encourage my kids to talk to me, to open up and tell me how they feel and what they think.

I've tried every way I can to encourage my kids to talk to me, to open up and tell me how they feel and what they think. By now, you're probably seeing that I've come pretty close to accomplishing this goal—so much so that sometimes, if I'm being honest, I may hear more than I want to know! Still, I keep those channels open. I want my kids to know they can tell me anything, ask me anything, show me anything, and I'll do my best to listen and answer with unconditional love.

No More Secrets

One thing I've learned from listening to the kids is how important it was to them, even as tiny tots, to believe they were hearing the truth from their parents—the real deal, the whole enchilada.

But what a challenge that is! How was I supposed to tell four-year-old Erin "everything" about the sin I'd committed while I was married to her dad? How was I supposed to manage the turbulent feelings that erupted between my ex-husband and me without whispering my anger and frustration to Don in the kitchen late at night? I did not know that six-year-old Jenni was lying over the heating grate in her upstairs bedroom, hearing every word! And how could I ever have known—until I learned the hard way—that to help my kids process the pain, I needed to keep bringing up the sore subject of the divorce again and again to make sure they knew the truth, told over time, in a little more detail according to what was appropriate for their age?

> *I needed to keep bringing up the sore subject of the divorce again and again to make sure they knew the truth.*

As one divorced mom said, "We can talk and talk and talk until they say, 'I don't want to hear it anymore!' And then in a few years they're grown up and saying, 'You never told me anything!'"

Don and I thought we had explained to our children as fully and as carefully as possible, given their ages, what we had done, how God had forgiven us, and how we'd been restored to our church. We thought it was all settled and we could move on. Sure, there were some things that weren't appropriate to discuss in front of them. And OK, we did resort to spelling out words and "speaking in code" occasionally, not realizing that some of our precocious kids were decoding the words but not necessarily understanding the full messages being exchanged. Apparently our lowered voices and surreptitious glances created an unintentional air of secrecy that somehow made the kids think we were holding back important information that was too terrible for them to know.

So one of the lessons I've learned—a little late—is that little eyes are watching and little ears are listening all the time, and what they think they see and hear may not be accurate. So, knowing what I know now, if I had it to do over again, I would try to re-create the atmosphere in our home during that time and take away the air of dark secrecy. And I would work even harder to spend time talking with and listening to my kids.

I've always valued those one-on-one times, but I've learned that really valuable heart-to-heart communication seems to defy scheduling. Sure, I could set aside time to go for ice cream with one of the kids, and while we would enjoy our time together, if the mood wasn't just right and the timing was wrong, the talking might be totally superficial.

Instead, I've learned to wait and watch for those perfect times when hearts open and the words pour out—like they did during that late-night talk with Erin when she shared her worries about not getting the full truth from her friend. Or like the day last week when the older kids came home for lunch and they were upset with one of their teachers.

I had a choice that day. I could've fixed their lunches and then gone into a quieter room to work. Or I could listen to them pouring out their hearts about the irritating teacher and enjoy feeling connected to them in a special "insider's" way.

Guess which choice I made.

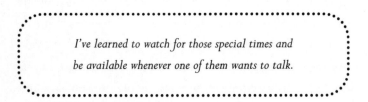

I've learned to watch for those special times and be available whenever one of them wants to talk.

I've learned to watch for those special times and be available whenever one of them wants to talk. Driving them to their various lessons, practices, and appointments used to be one of the best times to chat. Now that five of our teenagers (plus twenty-two-year-old Anna) are driving (pray for us!), they often drive themselves or each other wherever they need to go, so talk-time opportunities don't come as often as they used to. But I still watch for activities and moments when I think they might like to talk with me, and I do my best to let them know I'm available.

For example, Erin has always loved for me to wash her hair in the kitchen sink. It's just one of our things, and as strange as it may sound, we've managed to have some really great conversations as we lather, rinse, towel-dry, and comb out her silky long hair.

I've *always* loved talking with our kids, getting to know them better as they move into each new stage of their lives. So it still amazes me that, despite how close we are and despite all our heart-to-heart talks, there have been times when they've felt that I haven't been straightforward with them. That was one of the surprises when I started to work on this book. But to be honest, it wasn't the first time I'd been through that situation.

A little more than a year after Don and I married, merged our two families, adopted our sweet Sam, and happily headed off into a bright and promising future, a national television newsmagazine, ABC's *Primetime,* asked to do a story about us and our blended family. The kids got a kick out of having the TV cameras follow them around for a couple of days, and they eagerly urged their friends to watch the show the night it aired.

The program got rescheduled a couple of times, and when it was finally shown I was on the road and missed the broadcast. The segment included a couple of quick glimpses of the kids heading off to school—and then unleashed a full, unpleasant rehashing of the scandal that had marked the end of my first marriage and wrecked my career more than three years earlier.

We were blindsided by the show's focus, and I learned for the first (but certainly not the last) time how important it was for my kids to feel I'd been honest with them. The younger children were still mostly confused by all the uproar, but thirteen-year-old Anna was crushed, insisting that I'd never told her the truth about Don and me.

"We talked and talked and talked about it, Anna," I told her in a frantic phone call that night when I found out what had happened. "I thought you knew. I thought you understood."

"No, Mom," she said, her voice cracking. "I *didn't* understand. I *didn't* know. *You didn't tell me!*"

Distraught and remorseful, I hurried home, got a videotape of the broadcast, and took it and my kids to Pastor Lyon's office, where we watched it together and he gently helped the younger ones understand what it all meant.

Are you starting to understand why I've been so stunned recently to hear these children say *now* that they never felt they knew what had happened and what was going on? Sometimes I look back at all the ways we tried to help them understand, and then, when they insist that they were totally in the dark, I think, *Were we living in the same house? Did I slip into a different time warp somehow? How can this be?!*

The Kids' Top Ten List

The more we talked about what we all have learned during our years in the blender, the more excited the kids got about passing on their own helpful advice to others going through the process. They decided to put together a "top ten list," and I was thrilled that they offered it to me free of charge (if you can call a restaurant dinner for our family of ten plus assorted guests *free*). Interestingly, most of their suggestions are centered around communication, and all but one of them is aimed at the parents rather than the kids.

Donnie was the one who offered the choice bit of wisdom for children who are heading into a blended family: "Write your name on all your stuff." (Apparently there were a few ownership issues over toys and video games when he and Jonathan found themselves living in the same room.) He also adds this corollary: "Except don't let your parents write your name with a Sharpie on your white T-shirts." (I guess there was a bit of teasing from his friends when the name showed through. But honestly, when you have three kids who are all the same age and same size, what else can you do?)

So here are our kids' top-ten "rules" for parents, the absolutely essential steps parents have to take to help their children survive life in the blender. As you'll see, these suggestions apply to both the custodial and noncustodial parent:

1. Talk to your kids a lot about what's going on, even if you can't tell them *everything*. Make them feel like they know what's going on, even if there are details you can't share. And don't say, "You'll understand when you get older."

2. Don't lie. It'll come back to hurt your kids.

3. Don't talk about the other (noncustodial) parent. If you can't say something nice, don't say anything.

4. Keep your promises!

5. Live as close as possible to the other parent—ideally in the same city. (More thoughts on this in the next chapter.)

6. Be on time. (This one's especially hard for us folks who are chronologically impaired, but we try our best, remembering how crushed Donnie was on the big day he was to take his driving test and get his license. Don was so late picking him up that the place had closed by the time they got there.)

7. *All* the parents should have consistent rules and bedtimes for the kids. (I say, good luck working *this* one out!)

8. Eat meals as a family as often as possible, but at least once a week.

9. Keep the kids together. Don't split them up—for example, with the girls living with Mom and the boys living with Dad.

10. Be patient, and accept the fact that you and your kids are going to mess things up now and then. Be willing to admit your mistakes and apologize for them. The blending process takes time.

What Helped Most

I wish I could say Don and I scored a perfect ten on the kids' list, but by now it has to be obvious to you that we didn't even come close. But we did do one thing right. I think we all agree now that it's the thing that helped the kids most: we held fast to our faith. We kept a close connection with the church, and we encouraged our kids to be involved in their youth groups.

We did do one thing right . . . we held fast to our faith.

It's very hard for Christian couples to keep attending the same church when they divorce. Some people are able to do it despite the awkwardness, and my ex-husband and I tried for a while. On the weekends when I had the kids, they sat with me. On his weekends, they were with him. It was terribly uncomfortable for all of us, and as a result, I decided to try the new church I mentioned in the first chapter.

I was fortunate to find, on my first try, a church where I felt welcomed, loved, and nurtured despite all my past mistakes. You know, there are churches out there where you get the feeling that everyone in the congregation is perfect, or pretends to be. There are congregations where fallen Christians who make big-time mistakes are forced out, either officially or by the harsh attitude of the members. How blessed I've been that North Anderson Church of God has a different attitude. Its leaders and members operate by the standard that we're *all* sinners who "fall short of the glory of God, and are justified freely by his grace through the redemption that came by Christ Jesus" (Romans 3:23–24). As Don says, this is a church that "knows how to fix broken people."

> *This is a church that "knows how to fix broken people."*

They didn't simply acknowledge my past, pat me on the shoulder and say, "That's OK, honey," then pretend like nothing had happened. Instead, they assured me that God had heard my confession and had forgiven me for what I'd done—and they understood that I also needed an additional step. I needed to be restored to the fellowship of Christians. In *Broken on the Back Row,* I lay out the two-year process they shared with me to help that happen. It wasn't easy. I cried a lot of tears during that restoration and went through some very humbling encounters. But it was exactly what I needed to feel whole again.

While the adult congregation was helping me, my kids were being nurtured by some wonderful youth leaders in both our original church and then in our new one. Some were better than others, but eventually the kids found godly people who listened to them, guided them, encouraged them, and created worship times and activities that they enjoyed immensely.

Jenn was especially blessed by some of these leaders. She remembers one woman who took her aside and said, "I know you're going through a tough time. If ever you want to talk about anything, if you need someone to listen, I'm here for you. Here's my phone number. Just call me, and we'll go to Dairy Queen sometime."

And Jenn did exactly that. This woman became a special mentor to her, a confidant and prayer partner. And yes, sometimes I would drop Jenn off to spend time with her and think, *Gee, I wish that could be me. I wish Jenn could talk to me about what's going on in her life.* But at that stage in Jenn's life, she needed someone else, an objective third party, someone who could simply listen to what she said and acknowledge her feelings without feeling hurt by them. As Jenn says now, "If I was upset with Mom, I couldn't really go to Dad with it. And if I was upset with Dad, I couldn't go to Mom. I couldn't go to another kid because none of my friends had gone through a divorce and remarriage; they couldn't really understand what it was like."

The Importance of Youth Group

After spending time with our family and getting to know our kids, people have actually said to Don and me, "How did your kids turn out so great?"

I answer with two words: youth group. That's how important that link has been for us.

How thankful I am that devoted, caring, and knowledgeable Christians were available to my kids then—and that they or others are still playing a big role in our family today. The members and leaders of the youth group have made a major impact on our kids, and I thank God for them every day. Today they're like part of our family.

So my advice to you, when you're going through hard times that affect your family, is that you find a church where the youth group is strong, supportive, Christ-centered, and *fun,* and help your kids get involved in it. You might even want to help things along by taking the youth minister aside and saying, "I just want you to know that my child is going through a hard time right now. It would be OK for you to ask her how she's doing and see if she wants to talk about it." Sometimes even experienced youth leaders aren't sure what to say to a kid who's having a hard time—or whether to say anything at all—and that kind of comment can open the door of communication.

And think about this: it doesn't even have to be *your* church's youth group. You may feel you need to stay in a congregation that doesn't have a youth ministry—or doesn't have a strong group or has a group that doesn't appeal to your kids. Most youth groups welcome kids from all over the community and from other denominations. So ask around and also encourage your kids to ask their friends and schoolmates about youth groups in your area.

Also, if your church doesn't have a good youth group, consider asking your church leaders to get one started and then help in that work. Because our children were still pretty young when our families blended, Don and I got involved in the children's ministry, helping with the music program during youth meetings and events.

Reach Out to Others

I feel strongly that a good church is one that does more than offer its members a place to worship. A good church supports its members in their lives outside the church as well, providing support groups and organized volunteer services that reach out to those in need. For instance, among the many programs and groups our church sponsors is one that assists people who need long-term nursing care but don't have insurance.

Finally, I urge you to be aware of others who are going through what you've been through, and reach out to them. By helping others, you will help yourself. I have a friend who stayed in the same church through a painful divorce, and she said that she felt as though she had become invisible. "A lot of people knew what was happening, but no one mentioned it. It would have meant so much to me if someone had touched my shoulder and said, 'I know you're probably going through a hard time. I'm thinking of you and keeping you in my prayers. And if you need to talk, I'm here for you,'" she said. "Now I try to be that encouraging person, and it's been a blessing to me to know that I'm helping someone who's hurting."

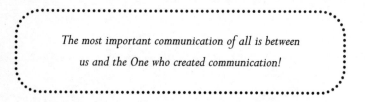

The most important communication of all is between us and the One who created communication!

Communication is so important when we find ourselves swirling around through the chop and mix cycles of becoming a blended family. We have to find ways to keep talking to each other and to those who can help us. And of course the most important communication of all is between us and the

One who created communication! He has given us a marvelous gift that can help us survive life in the blender. Whenever you're struggling to communicate with those around you, turn to Him. Talk to Him. And you'll find He will give you the right words when you need them, just as He said he would do in Jeremiah 1:9: "Now, I have put my words in your mouth."

4.

Trading Spaces

Always in Writing, Never in Stone

If I go up to the heavens, you are there;
>if I make my bed in the depths, you
>are there.
If I rise on the wings of the dawn,
>if I settle on the far side of the sea,
even there your hand will guide me,
>your right hand will hold me fast.

—Psalm 139:8–10

It was a great plan, or so we thought. After Don and I were married in Colorado with all our family and friends gathered around us, we stayed on in that beautiful Estes Park area for a few days of what we called our "family-moon." Then we headed back to the Midwest, and while my kids spent a few days with their dad and Don's kids visited their mom in Michigan, Don and I moved all of his family's things into the big white house my kids and I had moved into after the divorce.

We wanted to make the actual moving-and-blending process as painless for the kids as possible, so by the time they came back, everything was settled, and Don's kids' things were moved to our house. New bunk beds were installed, my kids' clothes were moved around to accommodate the clothes that were coming in, toys and games were neatly arranged on shelves, and life in the blender began.

My kids—Anna, Jenni, Jonathan, and Erin—were now joined by Don's kids—Donnie, Aly, and Mollie. As the oldest child, Anna got her own room, which we had created by renovating the attic. Jenni also got to keep her own room, although it was a room the other kids had to pass through to get to the bathroom, so it wasn't all that private. Donnie, who had suddenly gone from oldest to middle child, shared a room and a set of bunk beds with Jonathan. And the three youngest girls—Aly, Mollie, and my Erin—shared a single bedroom.

> *For a while, everything was rosy.*

For a while, everything was rosy. Then a few small skirmishes broke out, followed later by what sometimes sounded like a condensed replay of the Civil War. While there were plenty of peaceful and fun moments, specific rivalries quickly evolved. Although Donnie and Jonathan had been through a few unpleasant run-ins at school, their relationship flowed surprisingly well, and we were surprised that the loudest fighting occurred, not between the two boys, but between Donnie and Jenni. Somehow the two little eight-year-old dynamos managed to irritate each other by everything they did, beginning with breathing. Over the next few *years*, we would hear all sorts of yelling and screaming echoing down the staircase. A typical argument might sound like this:

"Mom! Donnie won't get out of my room. Make him get out!"

"Dad, she took my CD, the one I got in Michigan."

"This isn't your CD! This is mine. You loaned yours to Tommy."

This back-and-forth might go on a while, then we might hear a door slam or something hitting a wall, followed by, "Waaaaaaaaaaaah!"

"Is there blood?" Don might ask, standing at the foot of the stairs.

"Yes!"

Although most of these incidents were resolved *without* bloodshed, there were a few times when someone was "accidentally" hit by flying debris or someone got pushed and . . . Well, just let me say we *do* know the shortest route to the emergency room. Recently Jenn had to have some kind of medical exam, and she was told, "Oh! Your nose has been broken before." When she came home and told the family about it at dinner, she and Donnie argued about when it got broken and which one of their fights had caused it (although both incidents truly were accidents). Jenn said it happened "that time when we were fighting in the car."

"No, it was when we were arguing about what we were going to watch on TV," Donnie insisted. "*Twister* was coming on, and I was scared to watch it. I said turn it off. You said no, so we both ran for the clicker and I bumped you in the nose. I remember you had to stop the blood with one of Sam's diapers."

While Jenn and Donnie had some conflicts and felt confused and uncomfortable about the initial blending process, the three littlest girls seemed to do much better. Aly and Erin were six and five when Don and I got married, and they had become close while we were dating. As Aly says now, "At first it was like moving in with my best friend; it was fun, like one long party." Not that they didn't have their own squabbles occasionally as they adjusted from being best friends to becoming sisters. And then, as they got older and those adolescent hormones kicked in, there were more frequent spats. As Donnie says now with a weary sigh, "There were *so* many fights over whose bra it was."

And then there were the arguments over who sat where at the dinner table and who got to sit in the front seat of the minivan on the ride to school. Initially we had a rule that whoever got downstairs first each morning got the primo "shotgun" seat. But that caused too many knock-down-drag-out brawls on the staircase as two or more kids tried to edge out the others when they all got ready at the same time. Then Donnie started getting up early and coming downstairs twenty minutes before time to leave so he could holler, "Shotgun!" and get the good seat—a situation that incited great resentment among those who, as a result of Donnie's promptness, *never* got to sit up front.

The most important communication of all is between us and the One who created communication!

Things got so bad we eventually set up a "front-days" chart so each kid got a turn riding shotgun. It wasn't a simple chart, either, because there were too many kids and too few weekdays for each one to have a set day; i.e., Anna every Monday, Donnie every Tuesday.

Yes, many "adjustments" had to be made as we settled in together, but now, eleven years later, the yelling has pretty much stopped, and the kids have worked out a relationship that is, for the most part, harmonious. As Don says, "They argue, they fight, they fuss, but they also look out for each other and love each other. They're a family." It's interesting to me that some of our kids introduce each other now as "my stepsister" or "my stepbrother," but others, including Aly, Erin, and Anna, do not. "I stopped using *step* a long time ago," Aly says.

Maybe This Isn't a Blender Problem

As the kids were helping me put this book together, they shared stories (perhaps I should call them *confessions*) I'd never heard before. For example, there were mutterings about "that time Donnie hit Jenn with the telephone," and I was dumbfounded to learn that the *real* reason the security alarm had gone off when that upstairs window was mysteriously broken all those years ago was because someone threw the cat through it! ("Oh, he didn't actually go through it," one of them said. "He bounced off the window when it shattered.") And then there was the one about Jonathan falling out of his top bunk, hitting Donnie's broken arm that he'd stuck out over the edge because of the right-angle cast (a whole 'nother story right there), and *landing on the vacuum cleaner.* Apparently even now this is a story that cannot be fully told.

"He landed on the vacuum cleaner?" I asked, my head spinning from all I was hearing. "What was the vacuum cleaner doing in your and Jonathan's room in the middle of the night?"

"Oh. Uh. We, uh, we just liked to keep our room clean."

Sure. Two preadolescent boys liked to keep their room clean. I believe that, don't you? I'm thinking today that I would just like to know what was in the bag of that vacuum cleaner.

Or maybe I wouldn't!

Yes, those early days in the blender were pretty turbulent, sometimes bordering on Armageddon. There were times when Don and I sat in the kitchen, listening to the chaos raging above us, and thought, *What have we done? This will never work!*

It would have been so encouraging at that point if another experienced parent had come along and said, "Relax. This isn't about being a *blended* family. This is about being *any* family, especially a *big* family. Kids argue. Then they make up, and in a little while they argue again. It's just the way kids are."

(I can also imagine that parent then considering the ages of our tribe, looking into the future and realizing we would soon have *six* teenagers going through various hormonal stages, and saying simply, "God help you.")

If you're sitting at your kitchen table right now, reading this book while doors slam and kids' angry voices echo off the walls of your blended-family home, let me just pass that reassurance on to you now: it's going to be OK. In all probability, they're just being kids, and this has little or nothing to do with the fact that they're living in a blended family. Don't beat yourself up. Just do what you know to be right, use your best judgment, and have faith that this stage will pass.

Oh yes, and one more thing: *pray—a lot!*

Not So Fast

We know now that we *could* have made the blending process a little easier for our kids, possibly reducing some of the confusion and conflict that occurred. But we were operating under the best of intentions. We thought we were making things easier for our kids by moving all their furniture and possessions while they were off having a good time with their other parents. Then we welcomed them back home and happily gave them a tour of the new arrangements. Remember, we had all known each other quite awhile. In fact, some of our kids had known each other all their lives, either from going to the same school or from coming along occasionally when I was performing around the country and Don was traveling with the road tour as a backup singer. So it never occurred to us that we should have spent more time talking with them and working through the specifics of how we were all going to live together.

Now we know—because they've told us—we should have given them that "tour" *before* the actual move-in day. Even before the wedding. Jenn said recently that her advice would be, "Don't throw us together in one house in a day. Ease us in. They came in all at once, and I know it was weird for them because it was weird for us. It had been *our* house, and then all of a sudden these people we didn't really know were thrown in with us."

Even Aly, who was happy to move in with her best friend, admitted it *did* feel weird "to suddenly have all these brothers and sisters around all the time when I was used to just having one brother and one sister."

> *We should have asked for the kids' input and tried to accommodate their wishes or worked with them on compromises.*

We should have asked for the kids' input and tried to accommodate their wishes or worked with them on compromises. We should have helped them visualize what life in the blender was going to look like and feel like, for instance, taking them upstairs and saying, "Donnie and Jonathan, you will share *this* room. Your clothes will go here. Now, whose clothes should go on the right side of the closet and whose should go on the left? And who will sleep on the top bunk, and who will be on the bottom?"

There might have been some arguments at that point too, but we could have helped the kids see how to disagree agreeably and work out some compromises. Live and learn.

Change Day

Imagine being a little kid and living in a safe and secure place where every morning you wake up in the same room in the same house with the same people around you, and then your life is turned topsy-turvy and you have to move—not just once but several times a year, or even every week. Now you wake up in the morning, and it takes you a moment to remember which house you're in and which people are around you.

It must be *so* hard being a child enduring the upheaval of divorce. It's a painful thought that prompts me to remind parents in second marriages to keep in mind that the blending idea was *your* idea, not your children's. To them, it may seem like a tornado has roared through their lives, uprooting them and plopping them down in a strange new place.

In our blended family, we lived out various custody and visitation arrangements. None of them was good—there *is* no good way to do it. You *want* both original parents involved in their children's lives after a divorce; everyone agrees that's the best thing for the kids. But how do you do that without disrupting their lives and dragging them back and forth between households? Or how do you do that if one parent has only visitation rights and he or she becomes something like a favorite aunt or uncle who appears occasionally to take the kids to Grandma's for the day or who whisks them off to Disney World for the week?

There's no good answer. You just have to try to put the kids' best interests ahead of your own emotions and preferences and try to do what's right for them.

> *You just have to try to put the kids' best interests ahead of your own emotions and preferences and try to do what's right for them.*

Don and his first wife, Michelle, were able to manage their kids' living arrangements on a rather informal basis; they've never had a set schedule. They've just talked regularly about what would be best for them and for their kids, and that has worked well for them. The kids would live with Don in Indiana throughout the school year and would spend some holidays and parts of each summer with their mother in Michigan. They would spend birthdays and holidays wherever it worked out best in a particular year.

For my first husband and me, a more formal arrangement worked best, one that specified where the kids would be at particular times. For most of their growing-up years, they were with their dad every other weekend (usually Thursday night through Monday morning); then, on the weekends when they were with me, they spent Thursday evenings with their dad. We agreed that during even-numbered years the kids would be with me for their birthdays and specified holidays, and during odd years they usually would spend those days with him. When I was traveling, they usually stayed with him.

There were advantages and disadvantages to the formal and the informal arrangements. Don's kids had fewer of the unsettling, back-and-forth moves that my kids experienced every week. But because Don's children spent months at a time with their dad, and then with their mom, change day was a dreaded, tearful event as they said good-bye to the parent they'd been living with, knowing they wouldn't see him or her for a long time.

> *"I bawled my eyes out every change day," Donnie said.*

"I bawled my eyes out every change day," Donnie said. "I had a really hard time. There was a halfway point, a little town in Michigan that's two hours from here, two hours from there. I usually didn't get upset until we hit that town. Then I had to leave one car and get into the other. Usually I was screaming and crying. That was the hardest part."

Someone asked Donnie how his mom and dad interacted during those meetings and if change days were hard on his sisters too. "I don't know," he answered. "I just remember screaming." (I can assure you that they *were* hard for Aly and Mollie as well, and I can also tell you that, while Don and Michelle maintained a cordial and warm relationship, there wasn't a great deal of conversation while they carried or dragged their crying youngsters from one car to the other.)

I can hardly write about those scenes without feeling tears well up in my own eyes. I guess you would just have to call that kind of change day a "necessary evil," an unavoidable component of life in the blender. It did convince me to stay put, however, when people in the music industry urged me to move to Nashville after my divorce so that I could get my career back on track and have more convenient access to the music world's movers and shakers. I declined to do that; I needed to live in the same town as my children's dad, and I've never regretted that decision.

Because my ex-husband and I lived only a few blocks apart, change day for my kids wasn't nearly as traumatic as it was for Don's children. But the bad thing was, it happened *every week,* so it obviously disrupted their lives and took away some of their feelings of stability. The constant changing was especially hard on Jonathan, because he was (and still is) working through some learning difficulties due to a head injury that occurred when he was two (a bittersweet story told in more detail in *Broken on the Back Row*). Changes are hard for him, even now; but they were especially difficult then. And our arrangement was also hard on Jenni, the precious little Daddy's girl who adored her father. There were also times when various kids balked at having to change, not wanting to go back to the house of one parent or the other.

If you're riding the blended-family whirlwind right now, you're probably familiar with all these issues. You've probably seen the tears and heard the sobs that rip your heart in two on change day. And yet, as parents who love our children with the utmost devotion and concern, what else can we do but put them through this ordeal?

We love them, and we want them with us all the time, and yet most of us would quickly agree that we want the other parent involved in their lives too. We just have to trust God to guide us in doing what's right. And we prayerfully hope that whatever scars these tearful change days leave on our children, they will be soothed by the knowledge that they occurred because they were loved so deeply and strongly by *both* of their parents.

Personally, those difficult change-day memories have been eased somewhat by knowing that our older children now make their own arrangements to visit their other parent whenever it's convenient for them. Donnie drives himself to Michigan to visit his mother, and he says he holds no hard feelings about that little halfway-point town. "I stop there every time," he said with a smile.

Written but Flexible

Through the years and the tears, we've learned that the best way to share our children with their other parents is to be

flexible. It has helped tremendously to have a *written* schedule so we all know when the kids need to be where and what
we have all agreed to. Having it in writing helps alleviate
those "I thought you said . . ." arguments.

Even now I insist that all our activities and everything
we're doing must be recorded on a "written" calendar. I
have a bulletin board and a dry-erase marker board in the
kitchen—I call it Grand Central. Everyone's supposed to
leave me notes there, either tacked to the cork board or
written on the marker board. Then I add their events to the
calendar I keep on my computer, where it's easily updated.
I print out a new copy of the month's activities every time
something is added and post it on Grand Central.
Occasionally, when we have a lot going on, I distribute
copies to those I call the "heads of state": all the parents and
grandparents and other adults who help us stay on track.

At least that's how it's supposed to work. Recently I
called a family meeting to announce that I was tired of
being told at the last minute that someone had an event
that night and we all needed to be there. I didn't want to get
any more calls while I was out on the road from someone
who had forgotten to tell me about an appointment or a
meeting or something that required a parent's signature.

"That stuff drives me crazy," I said. "So remember: if
there is something important I should know about, *put it in
writing,* and stick it to that bulletin board in the kitchen. If
you think of something and realize, *I need to remind Mom*

about that, write it on the marker board. Is that clear? Does everyone understand? I will look at Grand Central and expect to find anything important you want me to know. Then I'll put it on the calendar and make sure you have a ride or a signature, or I'll be there to cheer for you if you're in some kind of event. But you've gotta give me some advance warning. Got it? IF IT'S SOMETHING I NEED TO KNOW, PUT IT IN WRITING!"

Then I went to the kitchen and started cleaning . . .

Later that night, when the house was quiet, I happened to walk by Grand Central and see a tiny piece of paper folded into a square and tacked up in the corner. On the outside of it, someone had written, "Mom."

When I unfolded it, this is what I read:

> *Mom, I love you.*
> *Sam.*

That's what he thought I needed to know.

OK, now, just let me . . . get a tissue . . . and dab my eyes a minute. (And they say my family meetings are worthless? That little note alone is priceless proof that they're worth every raucous minute of the chaos they generate.)

Obviously, having things written out can be very beneficial, not to mention rewarding! But even though a schedule should be established, I like to say it is "always in writing, never in stone." Meaning, things change. In fact, if I can throw out another cliché here, it would be that, for blended families, the only thing constant is change.

> *For blended families, the only thing constant is change.*

It's important not to let that schedule become an unbending third party that causes impediments rather than facilitating pleasures. Remember, when you're living in a blended family, you're no longer dealing with just two parents and a bunch of kids. Your family's schedule now may have to accommodate the schedules of two other complete families—four other parents (your kids' other parents and their new spouses) and *their* kids. You can see why things can get complicated quickly, even if they are written down.

Ideally the original mom and dad have a relationship in which they feel comfortable calling each other and asking if the schedule could change to accommodate special events and opportunities. Don and Michelle have always had that kind of relationship. Recently, when Michelle was diagnosed with cancer, we knew her kids wanted to be with her and she wanted them there. So we gladly changed our plans and arranged for the kids to spend the upcoming holidays with her and to be with her whenever their school schedule allowed. In fact, Mollie opted to move to Michigan and live with her mom while she's going through chemo and other treatments helping her make a strong recovery. Don and Michelle have always enjoyed flexibility in managing their children's schedule, so these changes weren't really anything out of the ordinary for them.

On the other hand, it took my former husband and me longer to get to that point. We needed more time for emotions to ease and tensions to be resolved. But now that we're there, it's *so* much better for us and for our kids. I'm sorry it couldn't have happened sooner, and if I had it to do over, I would do everything I could to acheive that kind of relationship. The kids no longer have set days when they live at his house, but he continues to be an important factor in their lives, and I am thankful for his devotion to them. Now that my career is getting back on track and I'm spending more time on the road, I try to make sure he always has a schedule of where I'm going to be and what activities the kids are involved in. He thanks me for doing that and says, "Don't worry. I'll be there—or I'll get them where they need to go."

The Crucial Stuff

One of the best bits of advice I can give you about moving your kids between two homes has nothing to do with emotions and everything to do with *stuff*. There are always crucial items that need to go everywhere the kids go as they are going back and forth: school papers that have to be signed, allergy medicine, soccer uniforms, and such.

> *Finally we came to the best solution: we used a bright red duffle bag, which we kept on the bench.*

At first we put each child's things in his or her little overnight bag or backpack. But if your kids are like mine, you too have learned that crucial things tend to disappear from such receptacles. Next we started putting *all* the crucial stuff in a red bin on a bench by the door so we would see it as we headed out. Finally we came to the best solution: we used a bright red duffle bag, which we kept on the bench. That way the crucial things didn't have to be transferred from the bin to the bag. They were always right there, ready to go.

A Prayer before You Go

While change day was always difficult, we did our best to give it a positive start. On those mornings, we all ate a big breakfast together, and almost always that breakfast consisted of homemade pancakes. (It's funny, but even to this day whenever we have pancakes someone will jokingly remark, "What? Is it change day?") At breakfast we would talk about the fun things the kids were going to do while they were with the other parent. Most important, we started that day with prayer, asking God to help us make change day go smoothly and to keep the kids safe and happy while they were away.

To be honest, in those early days, those prayers probably helped Don and me get through change day more than they helped the kids, because they were too young to understand. But as they grew, they came to feel God's "right hand" holding them fast, His love and presence giving them strength and courage, and they believed—they still do—that He is with them *everywhere,* as the beautiful psalm declares: "up to the heavens . . . in the depths . . . on the wings of the dawn . . . on the far side of the sea, even there."

Change day was a poignant, difficult day. And in some ways the parting got even harder after we adopted Sam and he got old enough to feel the loss of having his brothers and sisters suddenly disappear. Harder but bittersweet too, because while all the other kids are gone, we *do* have Sam to keep us company—and keep us entertained.

One morning when my kids had gone to the home of their dad and stepmother and Don's kids were in Michigan with their mom and stepfather, Sam came down to the empty kitchen, walked around the empty table, his stretched-out arm bumping along the backs of his siblings' empty chairs, and said sadly, like a kid who'd been shortchanged at Christmastime, "Mom, why don't *I* have any stepparents?"

5.

Good Cop, Bad Cop

Fair *Doesn't Always Mean* Equal

> Having children is like having a bowling alley installed in your brain.
>
> —Alan Bleasdale

When Don and I first blended our families, we resolved to treat everyone equally. We would do our best to see that no child got preferential treatment and everyone got the same loving attention, the same instructive guidance, and the same amount of goodies such as toys and video games. We would discipline all the children with the same voice, the same set of rules, and the same consequences when those rules were broken.

Seriously. We thought we could do that.

Then we realized that trying to treat everyone the *same* was driving us *insane*. It simply can't be done. You cannot treat eight children exactly alike; they are unique individuals, and each one needs a different kind of attention and discipline.

For example, Donnie and Jonathan shared a room when we first blended, and with both boys Don continued the nighttime tradition he had started when he and his children were establishing themselves as a separate family. Every evening about 7 p.m., Don would go upstairs and lie down on the bed (or sit on the floor beside the bunk beds) and talk quietly with the boys about their day or read a story, share a bedtime prayer, and then say good night. It wasn't necessarily lights out after that; it was just what Don called the evening wind-down. He did the same thing with his girls, Aly and Mollie, and their roommate, Erin.

When the boys got older, if they had finished their homework, they usually wanted to watch television in their room before they fell asleep. The problem was that Donnie would simply drift off to sleep with the TV on, but Jonathan wouldn't. We might get up in the middle of the night to use the bathroom and see that telltale light flickering under the bedroom door. We would go in to turn it off and find him wide awake, watching movies or infomercials!

It didn't seem fair to say Donnie couldn't watch a little TV just because Jonathan wouldn't turn it off. So we compromised: the TV could stay on until a certain time, then Jonathan had to turn it off (assuming Donnie had already fallen asleep). In exchange for doing this, Jonathan, who just didn't seem to need as much sleep as Donnie, was allowed to listen to his music, something he loved to do, provided he kept it turned down really low.

Meanwhile, we let Jenni set her own bedtime, knowing she might stay up until midnight watching a movie or reading a book. She always got her homework done first, and she always made A's. We figured we couldn't ever be harder on her than she was on herself, so we let her use her own judgment about how to use her nighttime hours.

It's one of those situations where it wasn't equal, but everyone accepted it as fair and appropriate.

Another example is that, from the beginning, Jenni and her older sister, Anna, had their own rooms, while, at first, the other kids had to share a room. It's one of those situations where it wasn't equal, but everyone accepted it as fair and appropriate. Anna was three years older than the twins and Donnie, and she needed a room where she and her friends could play their older-kid games and music. As for Jenni, she has always had a mother-hen kind of personality; she's someone who looks out for others and thus seems a little more mature than many kids her age. So the arrangement seemed like a commonsense way to give everyone the space he or she needed. As the kids have gotten older, and since we moved to a bigger house, the room assignments have changed so that in our current situation, those who want them have their own bedroom. The issue now is not who gets a bedroom. With all the drivers in our family now, it's (*gulp!*) who gets a car. We're still working on that one!

Knowing Whom to Ask for What

Just as we treat our kids differently according to what we think is appropriate for each one, our kids have sized up Don and me and know who to approach for which requests. As Don puts it, "They know who to go to when they want to go shopping, and they know who to go to when they're sharing something important that needs to be remembered."

> *Our kids have sized up Don and me and*
> *know who to approach for which requests.*

Folks, I'll bet you've guessed wrong about who's who in those categories. Don's the one they hit up when they want to go shopping. On the other hand, he readily confesses, "They know that telling me something is like writing it down in disappearing ink."

All the kids agree that I'm "tighter with money" than

Don is. As one of them confessed recently, "If Don's here and Mom's away, even if we don't clean our rooms when we're supposed to, we get our allowance. If Mom's here and we don't clean our rooms, then we get nothing."

(Room cleaning plays a large part in our discipline and financial conversations, as you'll see later. With all the talking we do about it, you might think the upstairs of our house is immaculate. You would be wrong. As Don says, we're still trying to find the carpet in most of those bedrooms; it seems like years since we've seen it, thanks to all the debris that's piled high most of the time.)

Anytime finances are mentioned, my kids say they have to pay more of their own way than Don's kids do. But here's how a typical conversation plays out. Jenn might say, "I went to Ecuador two years ago on a missions trip, and I paid for everything. I think Mom gave me ten dollars for spending money. Donnie went on spring break, and Don gave him a couple hundred dollars—just gave it to him."

But then I'll point out that, first, she'd been saving her money specifically to go on that missions trip since she was in fourth grade. And a lot of that saved-up money was *extra* money we gave her for Christmas and birthdays specifically for her missions trip. Plus, Jenn has done quite a bit of traveling to perform with me on the road. And when she does that, I pay her. This is a perfect example of why we say *fair* doesn't always mean *equal*.

In my mind, it all evens out. And when it doesn't, well,

that's between my kids and me and between Don and his kids. I don't think anyone could look at any of our children and say they've been deprived.

Discipline Yours, Love Mine

Picture this: two cute little seven-year-old boys, sitting nervously in the principal's office, awaiting their fate after being caught fighting on the playground. The principal walks in carrying what seems to the boys (who you've probably guessed by now were Donnie and Jonathan) to be a huge paddle.

Surely their hearts were pounding in their little chests as the principal questioned them about what they had done. Then, unexpectedly, the principal lifted his foot and smacked the paddle hard against the sole of his shoe with a terrifying *whop!* Both boys claim that even today they can still hear that heart-stopping sound echoing through the chambers of their memories. The principal didn't even touch them that morning, but the lesson was quickly absorbed just the same.

There have been rare but memorable times when Don and I have tried to muster that kind of stern and terrifying disciplinary presence in response to our kids' misbehavior. Don even re-created the paddle-the-shoe scene a couple of times. I was amazed that, as lovable as he is, he could strike fear in the heart of anyone, but he actually pulled it off.

(Remember, this is the guy the kids always want to go shopping with because he's such an easy touch for money! But whenever they find themselves on the other end of his disciplinary voice, they would run the other way if they could.)

I was amazed that, as lovable as he is, he could strike fear in the heart of anyone, but he actually pulled it off.

The other kids were reminiscing about one of those memorable disciplinary days recently. The incident started when the family was on an outing somewhere, and Donnie and Jonathan were bickering. The arguing escalated until Donnie smacked Jonathan on the arm, then Jonathan smacked him back. Don saw the whole thing and knew that Donnie had started the fight. He told Donnie he was getting a spanking when they got home.

Anna told Donnie recently, remembering that day, "You were almost frantic because your dad was gonna give you a spanking and you had never gotten a spanking before. We went to Target, but you stayed in the car, all upset and crying because you were going to get a spanking."

And then Anna added, "But you never did."

Donnie smiled and answered, "He didn't need to spank me. It took us so long to get home, and I was crying the whole time, I think he decided I had suffered enough, just *thinking* about getting spanked."

During our eleven years together we have taken turns being what our kids call "the heavy" when it comes to disciplining them. In the beginning, Don took on that role. "I guess I thought, as I tried to establish myself as the head of the household, I needed to play that role of the heavy," he said. "But maybe I was really trying to make us look like what the typical family looked like, and again, our family has taught us there is no *typical* family. Or if there is, we're certainly not it."

It was during this period of Don's "heaviness" (if you could see this fitness-loving, athletic husband of mine, you would know there's *nothing* heavy about him) that another incident occurred that still makes us laugh today. Don was at the kids' elementary school doing a wellness program for the YMCA. When he stopped by the principal's office to say hello, who should he find there but little ol' Donnie, sitting in the familiar hot seat again.

The part that makes us laugh now is imagining what both of their faces looked like as they spotted each other. There was Don, happily popping in for a quick hello before setting off to present his Healthy Kids program, and there sat Donnie, thinking, *Oh, no! This is THE WORST thing that could possibly happen!*

Apparently, very few words were said between the two, but once again, poor Donnie spent the day worrying himself sick about what would happen to him when he got home and Dad-the-Heavy got hold of him. Indeed, there was some stern talking, and there *were* consequences, but none of us remembers now what they were.

Don rather quickly relinquished the heavyweight title; it just isn't a part of his makeup to be the tough guy, especially when it comes to *my* kids. He happily admits now that the kids think of him as "the softie," the one who's most vulnerable to their whining descriptions of hardships caused by weeks that last longer than their allowance money or to their urgent requests to go to a movie "just this once" even though their room hasn't been cleaned as ordered.

Thinking that *someone* had to be the family heavy, I took up the role next—and all the kids say the title's still mine, which honestly bothers me because I see myself as the patient and understanding one. But more accurately, what has happened is that I'm the heavy for *my* kids, and Don's the heavy for his. Or, more aptly put, I'm the bad cop for my kids while he's the good cop when they're in trouble, and vice versa. It's one of the most valuable practices we've adopted as we've adjusted to life in the blender. When one of the kids misbehaves in some way—and honestly, this doesn't happen very often—then I'm the one who "hands down the sentence" for my kids, and Don serves as judge and jury for the "defendant." This applies to everyone but our adopted Sam, of course. He gets it from everyone! (But he's so cute he mostly gets hugs and kisses.)

Voice Lessons

It all comes back to the issue of communication. The fact is, I can say something to my kids in a certain way and a certain tone, but if Don says the same thing in the same tone to my kids, well, as much as we would like it to work the same way, it just doesn't. I don't like it. And he feels the same way when I use the stern "Mom voice" on his kids. I can tell Erin without batting an eye, "You aren't going *anywhere* this weekend until that room is clean," but it feels uncomfortable for me to say it that way to Don's kids, even after all this time. Their mother is a very important component of their lives, and I'm not her, nor am I trying to replace her. So it feels awkward for me to speak to them in that voice. If it's important to me that they clean their room, I might say, "Aly, I really need you to clean up your room before you leave, OK?"

I can say to Jonathan, "You're being a creep to Sam. Stop it. Knock it off," but if Don says that to Jonathan, my hair stands up on end. And he would feel the same way if I said to Aly, "Young lady, get up there and clean that room, or you can forget about going to the ball game tonight."

I know you're probably wondering, *So . . . what happens if the room doesn't get cleaned?*

Well, I might ask in a friendly tone, "Hey, Aly, did you get your room cleaned?" And if the answer is no, then I'll probably quietly ask Don later if he'll ask her to clean it. (The trick is not coming off like a nag, a whiner, or a tattletale, three roles I could be really good at if I let myself.)

If Don says something to Aly but the room doesn't get cleaned and she happily heads off to the ball game that night (because that may not have been part of his directive to her), then I'll probably drop it. I know I can trust Don to see that the room eventually gets cleaned—and that's what I really wanted anyway.

> *When it comes to discipline, I try to speak to my stepchildren in a different way than I speak to my own kids.*

The stepparent communication issue seems to be some sort of biological thing. I can say something to my kids, and it sounds authoritative rather than harsh, but the same thing said to one of my stepkids sounds like it's coming from the Wicked Witch of the West. I don't know why that's true, but for us at least, it is. When it comes to discipline, I try to speak to my stepchildren in a different way than I speak to my own kids, almost as I would to a close friend I'm upset with. Don similarly delivers discipline to his kids and stepkids.

This may not be the method Dr. Phil would recommend for maintaining "consistent" discipline in a blended family, but as someone who's actually *lived* in the blender for eleven years, I can tell you it's what works best at our house.

When it comes to *praising* our children, on the other hand, Don and I share a love for celebrating successes and encouraging hard work. We try to catch *all* our kids doing good things and then pour on the praise when it's deserved.

A good example of how we reward the positive began when our kids were little. It was quite an experience for us to take the kids anywhere and not cause a scene. Remember, they were all eleven or younger when we got married, and people would literally stop and stare as our herd passed by. Thus began the "compliment rule." We told the kids that if they received an *unsolicited* compliment about their good behavior, we would give each of them a dollar.

A bribe? you ask.

Heck yeah! We were willing to try anything. And you know what? It really worked. They loved "being good" and having a waitress or flight attendant tell Don or me, "I can't believe how well behaved your children are. We were rather nervous when you all walked in here, but what a refreshing bunch of children they are."

The kids would smile and grin at us with their halos shining ever so brightly. Then, once the complimenter left, eight hands would be held out to us, waiting for that dollar.

We didn't actually give them a dollar each time but kept it in an "account" that, oddly enough, resembled my purse. And then if they saw something in a gift shop or whatever, they would ask, "How much money have I earned?" I would tell them and let them spend their hard-earned money.

The compliment rule saved our sanity on many occasions.

Believe me, the compliment rule saved our sanity on many occasions. The kids still talk about it today, and when we all go somewhere as a group, someone (most likely Donnie), will yell, "Compliment rule in effect!"

It does feel good to look back on a few things and laugh.

A Conundrum of Clutter

The good cop–bad cop routine works fine when we're dealing individually with one of my or Don's kids, but when we've got a problem with *all* the kids, Don and I act together in a unified, effective, and memorable way. Or at least *we* think that's our style.

There was the incident of the cubby-dumping, for instance. There was a time, when the kids were little, when they went through a stop-and-drop phase. When they came into the house, wherever they happened to stop, that's where everything was dropped: backpacks, papers, snacks they were eating, shoes they were wearing.

So, thinking Martha Stewart style, we developed the idea of cubbies, a stack of cubbyhole boxes. Everyone would have a cubby in the mudroom, and that's where all the stop-and-drop stuff would go. The cubbies worked great—until they filled up. Then when the kids arrived home with all their stop-and-drop stuff, there was no place to put the new stuff because the cubbies were crammed with old stuff. So once again the house became cluttered with, well, clutter.

We called an emergency family meeting and announced that the cubbies *had* to be cleaned out.

But they were not cleaned.

Then we called another family meeting and said that the cubbies *would* be cleaned out—or else.

But they were not cleaned.

So one afternoon, right before the kids came home from school, Don and I took all the cubbies out to the driveway and dumped them. Just tossed all the stuff all over the place and waited for them to come home.

Here's the crazy thing. All our kids insist this incident never happened! They have no memory of it whatsoever, which leaves Don and me staring at each other with that deer-in-the-headlights look again, wondering, *Could we have dreamed this?*

Yet while the kids deny that it happened, we remember it so specifically—remember the specifics, that is, right up to the part about what happened when the kids came home and found their stuff in the driveway. Then the picture goes fuzzy.

The whole thing makes me wonder if maybe the kids didn't come home that day at all. Maybe we miscalculated and my kids were at their dad's that evening and Don's kids had some kind of lessons or practice or something. Is it possible that we stood there amid the rubble we'd dumped in the driveway, waiting for the light bulb to come on in our brains telling us that we had done the cubby dumping on the wrong day? It might just be that the frustration of having to clean up that mess ourselves was so great we simply erased that part from our memories!

At any rate, since the whole thing was done as a discipline lesson for our children, it's rather deflating that they don't even remember it. But it *must* have happened, because I do remember that, at least for a while, whenever Don or I would ask the kids to pick up their "junk," they would run, not walk, to gather their belongings and take them to their room. Ah, sweet rewards.

Choose Your Battles

Disagreements about discipline can cause big problems in blended families. It took us quite awhile to find a system that works for us, but there's no doubt that the "love-mine-discipline-yours" approach is it. And while we agree that we will each be the primary disciplinarian for our own biological children (plus our adopted Sam), Don and I have also done a lot of talking and thinking about the overall issues in which discipline is most important to us. On those issues, we're definitely on the same page.

For instance, I may talk a lot about getting the kids to clean their rooms and pick up the clutter, but truth be told, that's not a battleground issue for us. We see that the kids keep their rooms clean enough to keep the board of health at bay, and basically we leave it at that.

We feel a lot stronger on other issues such as keeping their grades up, being respectful of us and each other, being truthful and trustworthy, and maintaining good character. When someone crosses a line and violates our standards in those areas, there *will* be consequences, and they *will* be enforced. If one of Don's kids gets grounded for making a D on a report card when we were told throughout the grading period that everything was fine, all homework was done, and all tests had earned high marks, then he or she doesn't need to come sidling up to me trying to get a day pass when Don is out of town. It ain't gonna happen! And the same is true if one of my kids violates my trust and a punishment is imposed. Don will stand firmly with me on enforcing those restrictions.

On the other hand, there *are* times when we've been known to bend the rules a bit. For example, my Jenni is currently ranked third in her high school class. She's a great student who works hard. In fact there were times, when she was younger, that she would actually ask her elementary-school teachers for extra work!

There are times when we've been known to bend the rules a bit.

She's still making straight A's today even though she's involved in a lot of extracurricular school and church activities. Sometimes, because of all the work she's doing, she needs what we like to call a "mental health day." So when she calls and says, "Mom, could you call the school and get me out for the afternoon? We're just doing a review in that class, and I'm already prepared for the test," then I make that call and ask that she be excused. Jenni comes home and takes a nap or just hangs out with me. It's good for both of us.

Recently she told me, "I can see it from both standpoints, and I know it wouldn't work for everyone. [In some schools, students are dismissed from final exams when they maintain perfect attendance.] But for me, it's been really beneficial that you've let me skip sometimes."

I'll do it occasionally for my other kids too, and so will Don. But only if those kids have proven themselves trustworthy. As I've said, I'd better not call in an excuse for you and then find out later that your grades have dropped! But I do recognize that there are some days when school just may not be the most important thing in a child's life. Sometimes, when you have a mom who's away from home a lot, as I am, just getting to stay home awhile and hang out with her may be more valuable, in the big picture, than another class review.

"Discipline is dicey," one stepparent said recently, and I certainly agree. It's one of the biggest challenges of surviving life in the blender.

6.

May I See Your ID?

Meet the Ganisilapivys

For you created my inmost being;
    you knit me together in my mother's womb.

               —Psalm 139:13

It was such an innocent comment. Who would have thought it could provoke such a torrent of emotion?

Less than a year after we were married, Don and I took our blended family on our "familymoon phase 2," a trip for the nine of us (this was pre-Sam) to Myrtle Beach for the first of many annual family vacations. One day, when it was time to leave the hotel and head out to the beach, Don cheerily called out, "Let's go, Peslis family!"

That's all it took for my four kids, whose last name is Helvering, to stage a loud and raucous revolt that rattled the rafters and taught all of us a crucial lesson: each of us has a name, and that name is important to us.

"We are *not* the Peslis family!" one of my kids yelled. "We are Helverings, and our mom uses her maiden name, Patty, and that's Nana and Papa's name, and *we are not Peslises!*"

> *Poor Don stood there looking like he'd just been dipped in water and plugged into a light socket.*

Poor Don stood there looking like he'd just been dipped in water and plugged into a light socket. "I'm sorry," he said humbly. "I just wasn't thinking. You're absolutely right." He looked at all the young faces staring back at him with various expressions ranging from his kids' bewilderment to my kids' defensive anger. "This is something we need to talk about, isn't it?"

So we talked. And talked. And talked. And talked. Everyone agreed that Don couldn't be expected to say, "Let's go, Peslis and Helvering and Patty family" each time he was trying to herd everyone out the door. But what *could* he say? We needed a new name—a nickname. We first tried variations using parts of all three names, coming up with things like Pesverpatty and Helverpatlis and even Helplis, but somehow those names just didn't have the pizzazz a brilliant and dynamic family like ours needed. Finally we wrote the letters of all our names on slips of paper and drew them out of a hat (OK, it was a brown paper lunch sack) until we came up with the nickname we've all loved and claimed as our own for more than ten years now. We are . . . the Ganisilapivys.

What's in a Name?

Sometimes the biggest lessons come in the smallest moments, and that's what happened to Don and me that day. That incident was the spark that helped us realize how important our identity really is to each of us as individuals, and also as members of our big blended family. We all need to feel that we matter, that we are recognized and cherished for those specific talents and traits that create our unique personality. That we each have a history different from everyone else's history.

It was a true light-bulb moment for us, one we now look back on with amazement, wondering why we didn't think of it earlier.

As our kids would say, "Duh!"

Since then we've worked hard to champion the uniqueness of each one of our kids, and of ourselves and our family as well. As Anna put it, "Each child in a family, but especially in a blended family, needs something that is uniquely their own, that only they can claim." We continue to work hard to identify those unique characteristics, and as we've recognized the individuality of each family member, we've done our best to help find an outlet for his or her specific talents and aspirations. Those individual needs were played out last year when it was time to plan summer activities. It would have been a whole lot easier if everyone had just wanted to go to the same summer camp, but that wouldn't have allowed for individuality. So here's how the summer played out instead:

Anna worked full time in marketing and public relations for IOPO, the Indiana Organ Procurement Organization. Among other things, the group publishes brochures given to Indiana residents when they sign up for a driver's license. Donnie, Jonathan, and Mollie went to Florida for Big Stuff, a wonderful worship experience geared to students in junior high and high school. Erin and Aly went to church camp here in Indiana. Jenn was part of a youth convention called Student Venture held at the YMCA of the Rockies in Estes Park, Colorado, where Josh McDowell was one of the speakers. Then Jenn and Aly went to Russia as part of a program our church offers. Sam spent his summer playing all-stars baseball, and I don't mean just a game or two a week. That kid seemed to be at the ball field 24/7!

In this chapter, I'd like to share with you some of the unique characteristics of the Ganisilapivys, hoping these descriptions will spark your own search to identify those special traits and talents that make your blended family, and each person in it, a wonderfully unique creation of God. I'll start off with Don and zip through the kids in alphabetical order. We usually go in order of age when we're talking about the kids, but this time we thought we'd mix it up a little bit (although, if it makes me think too much, I may just start over and do it the old way).

Don. Besides being the world's best husband and dad, Don is a talented musical artist. He sang professionally for many years, including a stint with Voices of Liberty, one of the resident groups that performs daily at Disney World in Florida. He has a magnificent voice, and I love it when he can travel with me and join me on stage for a song or two. His main focus now, however, has shifted from music to a rather new educational field called character development. He completed his master's degree in education in that subject last year and is employed at Anderson University, where he is the director of the Center for Character Development. Besides working with future teachers, he is the community liaison for the public schools in our area. He is just awesome at his job, and we can't go anywhere in town without somebody stopping us and wanting to chat. He knows everyone, and everyone knows him.

He is truly the love of my life, and I thank God every day that this romantic, fun-loving, athletic, handsome hunk of a man is my husband. I'll tell you a little more about Don's unique history in the next chapter.

Aly. Don's oldest daughter, Aly, has a creative streak that's unmatched in the rest of the family. We first noticed it one day after we'd all moved in together and Aly, Mollie, and Erin were sharing a bedroom. Aly led the girls in playing beauty shop with their Barbies, and they ended up "styling" all the dolls' hair by, well, they cut it all off! It was a little traumatic at first, especially when we thought of how much all the dolls had cost, but it turned out to be a stepping-stone of sorts for Aly, because now we all ask her to help us with our hair when we really want to look our best.

> *As a little girl, Aly was always happiest if she could be making something with her hands.*

As a little girl, Aly was always happiest if she could be making something with her hands. She loved to get off by herself and work on one of her projects, whether it was drawing, making jewelry, working on a costume for show choir, or completing some other crafty creation. Soon after our families blended, she asked for her own room, and we could see that she wasn't asking because of any hard feelings or resentment toward her younger sisters. She was simply getting older and needed private space to work out her creative ideas without being bothered by her siblings. So we did some rearranging and updated the attic to give Aly her own special, secluded space. She loved it.

She ventured into a new area last year and entered the high school solo musical competition for the first time, singing an amazing rendition of "Someone Like You" from the Broadway show *Jekyll and Hyde*. She also started up a little business decorating messenger-bag purses that are oh, so clever and fun.

Aly, now seventeen, wants to be a missionary when she grows up, and believe me, she's going to be a good one, given her love-filled heart for God and her passion for sharing the gospel. The most amazing thing this rather shy, introspective young lady has done recently is start a Bible study group— all on her own. The group has grown to fifteen or so kids now, all but one of them from other churches, and they meet every week with Aly serving as the leader.

Anna. My firstborn, Anna (we pronounce it *AHN-uh*), now twenty-two, will graduate from college this year and move on to that next big step: marriage. I'm still struggling to accept that she's all grown up. I remember her as a little girl so full of life that she just didn't want to take time to sleep. She had a real hard time at night going to bed and *staying* there. I would lie beside her and read her a story, kiss her good night, then head for the family room to wind down and watch a little TV, but she would pop back up and party on.

One night Anna kept getting up and coming into the TV room saying she just wasn't sleepy. This happened several more times until finally she came down and said, "Mommy,

I know you said to go to sleep, but it's not my fault. My insides keep telling my feet, 'We want to *play!*'"

There wasn't much left to do but giggle and smooch and snuggle with that lovable little manipulator. No! I didn't just write that, did I? But maybe that's why she is making a career out of public relations. She's recognized throughout our family as having a special gift for, shall we say, enthusiastic chitchat. As Jenn says about her big sister, "Somehow Anna could talk you into paying fifty dollars for an ugly, ordinary cardboard box, and then afterward you would ask yourself, *Why on earth did I buy that?*"

She has the friendliest, most upbeat personality of any of us and makes those around her feel special. She is also our family's ballerina. She has taken dance lessons all her life (and now teaches them) and says that dance was her "therapy" during those stirred-up days of divorce and remarriage. I love it when she comes along to perform at my appearances, dancing while I sing "Anna's Song," which was written especially for her. Other times she serves as my fill-in road manager when my usual crew is shorthanded. She's good at it, because she spent years on the road with me as a little girl.

Anna's history includes a funny story about her nursery-school days. One day when the class was going to make pancakes, the teacher went around the room asking the students what ingredients they would use. As her classmates answered confidently, "flour," "sugar," "eggs," Anna got increasingly irritated. Finally she raised her hand and said, "No, this is how you make pancakes: you get them out of the freezer, put them on a plate, cook them in the microwave, put syrup on them, and eat them." Then she added emphatically, "*That's* how you make pancakes."

When her teacher told me that story I thought, *Hmmmm. Maybe we've spent a little too much time on the road living in an RV!*

As this book goes to press, Anna is looking forward to two big events: graduating from college and getting married. Her fiancé is a fine young man named Collin Trent, and he is both handsome and charming. In fact, you might call him Prince Charming, because that's what he is to Anna—her dream come true.

Anna and Collin attended nursery school together, but they didn't start dating then. No, indeed! I put my foot down and said, "Anna, no dating until you're at least five!" Just kidding. In fact, although our families have known each other for years through church and other activities, Anna and Collin didn't really "discover" each other until they were seniors in high school. Then, even though it wasn't love at first sight (since they'd known each other for at least a dozen years), it *was* definitely love.

They both attended Anderson University and dated steadily throughout all four years there. During that time, Collin has become a member of our family. Yes, technically he "belongs" to Anna, but he has won over the hearts of the rest of us too. He obviously has lots of patience and a fun-loving spirit, because he already has survived several Ganisilapivy vacations. And he's so handy to have around. Just like Jonathan has an invisible keyboard in his head, Collin apparently has an invisible Palm Pilot embedded in his brain. Tell Collin any date in any year, and he can instantly tell you what day of the week it was or will be! No wonder his presence is now required at all our family meetings and other planning sessions.

Shortly before Christmas 2004, Collin asked for our blessing to marry our sweet Anna. I cried and laughed and hugged him as I loudly answered, "Of course!" They wisely set a date for after their college graduation, and we are all happily looking forward to summer 2006, when those wedding bells will be ringing and our family will be in off-the-charts celebration mode.

We've all been excitedly "helping" Anna with the wedding preparations. You don't think all the girls in the family could let her pick out a bridal gown all by herself, do you? Of course not! We all had to go. During our outing, Anna asked her sisters if they had had any advice for her. All they said was, "Just don't become a psycho bride." Isn't that touching?

Donnie. I've already told you that Donnie is the family comedian, a trait he says he got from his mother, who he describes as "one of the funniest people on earth." In the middle of a tense moment or a heated discussion, he can throw out a little zinger and change the whole atmosphere in the room. And, he points out modestly, he has "incredibly good looks."

He has a great voice but especially loves to play the drums. Last year Donnie put together a band called Farraday with some friends, including Jonathan as lead singer and Donnie on drums. At our local Battle of the Bands competition, would you believe this first-time group won third place out of a field of twelve competing bands? They're on a roll!

Don is helping Donnie reclaim the position he gave up when our families blended and he moved from first to fourth.

Something wonderful happened to our family a couple of years ago (more about that in the next chapter), and as a result of it, Don has started calling Donnie "Number One" because he is, after all, Don's firstborn child. Don is helping Donnie reclaim the position he gave up when our families blended and he moved from first to fourth. It doesn't mean we suddenly pretend he is older than Anna, Jennifer, and Jonathan. It just means, for Don as a dad, Donnie was first, and Don wants to acknowledge and celebrate that fact. It's been good for Donnie, now eighteen, to hear it.

Don has made a special effort to do things with Donnie, just the two of them, as though there weren't two other kids his age in the family. Last year they took scuba lessons together, and guess what: Donnie was better at it than Don was. There at the bottom of the pool with their gear on, it was Donnie who learned first how to use the hand signals to communicate effectively with his dive partner. And if Don was a little slow to figure out how to use a piece of equipment, Donnie was there helping him get the hang of it. The experience was a transforming one for both of them.

One night Donnie came home and shared this funny and meaningful story with us. He reminded us that he had been a quick study in learning the underwater hand signals, but his dad wasn't so fast. They were both at the bottom of the pool, and Don was using some signals Donnie hadn't seen before. He wasn't sure what Don was trying to tell him with his exuberant waving and pointing but thought it might be something like, "Good job," or "How cool is this to be down here with you?" or "I'm so proud of you." No, it wasn't anything like that. Don told us later he was trying to tell Donnie he had an enormous cramp in his leg and needed help. We all got a kick out of that.

In scuba, Donnie and his dad are equals (now that they've learned to communicate), and Don is thrilled to see his bright and witty son become a smart and caring young man.

Erin. Just as Don has made Donnie feel special by calling him "Number One," I've started calling sixteen-year-old Erin "my baby" again. When our families blended, Mollie retained her position as youngest and Erin moved up to next-to-youngest. Then we adopted Sam, and Erin was nudged closer to the middle-child position. I've always told Erin she will always be *my* baby, because she was the last child I gave birth to, but as she got older, I said it less and less, thinking a teenager wouldn't want that designation. But I was wrong. Being your mom's "baby" implies a sweet innocence, a cherished relationship, and those words perfectly describe Erin and me. She loves it when I call her my baby, and I plan to do it until she's at least seventy-two.

There's nothing babyish about Erin's character, however. She is a young woman who has set her own style and her own priorities, and one of those priorities is to carve out her unique niche. That's why, when she started high school two years ago, she decided to go to the *other* school in our town, not the one her older siblings were attending. She didn't want to follow everybody else; it was important to her to do something that was uniquely hers, and she made a great transition.

Again, it would have been a whole lot easier for us if *all* the kids attended the same school. But we understood why Erin wanted to do it, and we were impressed that she stuck to her decision, even when her siblings sounded off with a lot of criticism about the rival school. They pointed out that when Erin joined the new school's show choir, she would be competing against Jenn, Jonathan, Donnie, and Aly, who were active in *their* school's show choir. I'm sure it was a bit intimidating for Erin, but she had an awesome year. At many show-choir competitions, judges pick one singer from each choir who performs exceptionally well. My little Erin received this award two out of three times her first year.

It was a busy, busy time, but we survived it—and enjoyed the two schools' many events. Then, at the end of the year, something surprising happened. Donnie and Aly decided they wanted to change schools too and finish out their senior year at "Erin's school." Imagine that! At first we were skeptical, thinking it was a whim. But, like Erin, they wanted to assert their choice. When they laid out their reasoning—among other things, that they wanted to go to school with friends from our church, kids they felt strongly about and said they needed in their lives—we realized they had thought things through and had laid out a plan. We said OK, and although it has added even more chaos to the family calendar, we are enjoying every minute of it.

> *Eighteen-year-old Jenni is more dedicated to perfecting her music gift than anyone else.*

Jennifer. Ours is a musical family, but all of us Ganisilapivys agree that eighteen-year-old Jenni is more dedicated to perfecting her music gift than anyone else. As Donnie said, "All of us can do it, but Jenni's the only one of us who really works at it. She's one of the hardest workers in music I've ever met in my life." (And you know if *Donnie* says this about the sibling he bumped heads with most often when our families blended, it *has* to be true!) Jenni has a diligence and a discipline to refine her music that inspires all of us, and it has paid off in many ways, including winning a national solo competition.

She wants to use her music to carry the gospel message to others, and when she decided not to participate in her high school's show choir her senior year of high school so that she could "get more involved in the activities at my church," one of the kids asked incredulously, "How could you get any *more* involved than you are now?"

For years Jenn has traveled with me when her school-work allowed, and wherever she sings, the audience is amazed. She had her first paid performance (at a youth convention in Cincinnati) when she was just fifteen. This year she's part of the worship team with Women of Faith's Revolve tour, and she has a blast up there on stage, singing her heart out and sharing her love for the Lord.

She's not only an outstanding performer, she's also a gifted mentor, probably because she's had so many older mentors in her own life. Now she has a heart for reaching out to junior-high girls. "I want to mentor them like the mentors who helped me," she said. "I want to be the person they can go to when they find themselves in a crazy situation."

While the kids and I were talking about this book and

they were helping me identify each one's unique talents and traits, Aly paid Jennifer the highest tribute, illustrating how contagious Jenn's love for God really is: "Jenn has been one of the reasons I have stayed strong in the church," Aly said. "She's one of the reasons I want to be a missionary." Earlier I talked about pop-up pain, but honestly, there is pop-up joy too, and this is a great example of it. When you least expect it, there it is. What a sweet gift Aly's words were to Jenn—and to her family as well.

Jonathan. While Jenni works hard at polishing her musical gift, her twin brother, Jonathan, just opens his mouth and amazes us all. He has an awesome range of natural musical abilities, including what is called "relative perfect pitch." That means when our family is singing together, we can ask Jonathan to hum whatever note we need to get us started, and he nails it every time. If we need a middle C to start off the song, Jonathan can access that astounding invisible keyboard in his head and give it to us. That's the perfect-pitch part. But when people sing a cappella, even the best musicians inevitably go flat. Someone who has *perfect* perfect pitch can't go flat with them, so he or she ends up sticking out and sounding like someone making a mistake. Jonathan has *relative* perfect pitch that lets him "adjust his head," as we say, and go off-key with everyone else (although it probably pains him to do it).

He also has the amazing ability to sing a single part, solo. He doesn't need to hear the other parts—soprano, alto, baritone, bass—in order to sing the tenor part. If you want to hear what that part, and that part alone, sounds like, Jonathan can sing it to you.

He has nurtured these musical gifts while overcoming some serious obstacles. When Jonathan was a not-quite-two-year-old toddler, he pulled a heavy coatrack—a hall tree—onto his head. The impact fractured his skull, and one of the metal hooks pushed the skull fragments into his brain. The accident and the emergency surgery that followed were terrifying experiences for all of us, but Jonathan was treated in Indianapolis by a highly skilled neurological team, and they brought him through the fire and gave him back to us. Since then he has worked hard to cope with some learning disabilities, and he still has some residual effects from the accident, but as I write this, he is preparing to take his driver's test, and he has blossomed into a dedicated student as well as a gifted musician.

With the kids separating into two different high schools last year, and with Jenni deciding not to participate, Jonathan was left alone to perform in his school's show choir. He is a rather shy young man who is "happy in his own company," as they say. So I was a little nervous about his being alone in show choir, where always before he'd had Jenn or Donnie or Aly to speak up for him and look out for him. Let me just say that this was *my* fear, not Jonathan's. When it was obvious that he no longer had the luxury of having siblings who would tell others how he felt about things, he stepped up and accepted the challenge. In fact, he became a leader within the group, showing self-confidence and forthrightness we never knew he had. It's been a remarkable transition, one that has truly amazed all of us, even Jonathan.

And there's something else that's extra-special about Jonathan. He is the most supportive young man you could ever meet. As Jenn said, "If someone beat Jonathan in some kind of competition, Jon wouldn't even think twice about it before being 1,000 percent supportive of that person who beat him. He would congratulate him, be happy for him, and cheer for him in the next round. He is consistently supportive of his friends, his family, and his competitors. We can always depend on him for that."

> *"If someone beat Jonathan in some kind of competition,*
> *Jon wouldn't even think twice about it before being*
> *1,000 percent supportive of that person who beat him."*

Mollie. The prize in our family for being the most selfless has to go to Mollie, now fourteen. For years, this adorable youngest member of our blended family charmed us with her sweet smile and caring attitude. Then, a couple of years ago, her mom, Michelle, who lives in Michigan, was diagnosed with cancer. It would have been easier for Mollie to stay in Indiana where she had grown up with her big blended family of brothers and sisters. But that wasn't Mollie's way. In her unique, caring style, she wanted to be with her mother to support her through that difficult experience—and to help care for her little half-sister, Sydney.

So Mollie moved to Michigan, and I know Michelle is ever so thankful to have her own sweet "baby" with her, just as I love having mine with me.

Donnie says, "Mollie is the pick of the litter." Then he adds, "No offense, Aly."

When our family gathered to identify each other's unique characteristics, these are the words I heard when we talked about Mollie: "kindest," "sweetest," "gentlest," "most sincere," "most admired." She is, in short, a wonder child, and she inspires us all. We love having her back for visits, and of course she always joins us for those wild Ganisilapivy summer vacations.

Sam. In the next chapter, I'll tell you more about how God brought Sam into our lives, but for now I'll just say that we are all *very* thankful He did! Soon to be ten years old, Sam is an athlete, a live wire, an encourager, and a jokester (apparently Donnie is training Sam to be the next family comedian). And he is oh, so creative. When he was younger, he named all his toys Tylenol, and he begged Don and me for a baby sister or brother he could name Tylenol too. (The furthest he got with that request was a boy doll.) I'm not sure why he loved that name so much; maybe it just felt good on his tongue!

Sam definitely is following Don's footsteps as someone who loves sports and fitness. Last summer during one four-game series of all-stars baseball, Sam was at bat twelve times and hit the ball twelve times, and he made it to first base ten out of the twelve. Move over, Sammy Sosa!

Celebrating Each One

Putting this chapter together, recounting each of our children's unique characteristics, has been an exercise in awe and thanksgiving. How wonderful these eight young creations are! What a blessing each one of them has been to my life—and yet how different each one is, touching my heart and inspiring my mind in his or her own specific style.

I first started thinking this way a few years ago, around Thanksgiving. It was a beautiful starlit evening, a perfect fall night. I had just gotten off my tour with Chonda Pierce, and it always takes me a few days to connect with each of the kids after I come off a long road trip. I had been praying that God would give me a window of opportunity to have a special moment with each one of the kids, and sure enough, He did. I had some time with Donnie to help him find the Christian Comedy Association on the Web. I had a chance to visit with Aly about a misunderstanding she'd gone through with some girlfriends. Jonathan and I slipped away to see a movie, and I found little tidbits of time with Anna, Erin, and Sam as well. I wouldn't trade anything for those awesome moments.

But back to that perfect night. I had picked up the kids from their show-choir rehearsal, and as we drove home we oohed and ahed about how clear the sky was and how many stars we could see. When we got home, Jenn and I stayed outside; we turned off all the outside lights and stood in the driveway a long time, looking up. Just looking and talking. We talked about God and how amazing it is that He created all this. Then, for some reason, Jenn asked, "Mom, which way is north?"

I pointed in the direction I thought it was. Honestly, I'm directionally impaired, and under most circumstances I wouldn't have a clue which way north is. But standing in our driveway, I knew which way to go to Alexandria, where Bill and Gloria Gaither live, and that's north of our home. So we both turned that direction, and as we did, we saw the most beautiful falling star. It was so big and clear. In the past when I've seen falling stars, I've caught a glimpse out of the corner of my eye, making me wonder if I'd really seen it. But not *that* falling star. We watched it fall for a good three seconds. We couldn't believe it. It was so stunning we both whooped and shrieked, prompting our dogs to start barking hysterically, probably thinking we were being attacked by an ax murderer. We laughed and hugged and cried, all at the same time. Then we ran inside in case the neighbors came out to see what all the commotion was.

What a moment. A beautiful moment with my beautiful daughter . . . and our wonderful God. It was almost like He knew we had been admiring and appreciating His creation all evening. Isn't it just like God that He would seem to say, "Thanks for noticing. How about a falling star to top off the evening?"

It's the same way when we notice and appreciate the unique characteristics that make each of our children special. It's easy, in a blended family, to want to meld all those unique traits into one homogenous mix. It's easier if we all think alike and act alike. But that's not the way God created us. He put together a special group of genes and chromosomes just for me—and another special group just for you. He made us with as much care and creativity as He made everything in creation, from worms to stars. Then He turned it over to us. Amazing.

This beautiful passage from Psalm 8 puts it into powerful perspective:

I look up at your macro-skies, dark and enormous,
 your handmade sky-jewelry,
Moon and stars mounted in their settings.
 Then I look at my micro-self and wonder,
Why do you bother with us?
 Why take a second look our way?

May I See Your ID?

Yet we've so narrowly missed being gods,
    bright with Eden's dawn light.
You put us in charge of your handcrafted world,
    repeated to us your Genesis-charge,
Made us lords of sheep and cattle,
    even animals out in the wild,
Birds flying and fish swimming,
    whales singing in the ocean deeps.

GOD, brilliant Lord,
    your name echoes around the world. (vv. 3–9 MSG)

7.

Not Just Yours,
Not Just Mine—*Ours*

And Now for Something Completely Different

For we are God's masterpiece. He has created us anew
in Christ Jesus, so that we can do the good things he
planned for us long ago.

—Ephesians 2:10 NLT

hen you blend two families, especially two families
with small children, you have to prepare yourself to hear a
lot of "No! Put that down! That's *mine*!" and "That's *my*
game! Who said you could play it? Mommmmmmmm!"

Of course you hear plenty of that among blood-related
siblings in other families too, but when two families blend,
kids (and adults) can't help but feel an even stronger urge to
defend their territory and their stuff. Before the blending,
that child or adult has been in relatively complete control of

whatever the thing is, and now other people are roaming around picking it up, playing with it, moving it, using it, taking it.

"Put that down!" Pick that up!" "Give that back!" "Don't touch that!"

"Mommmmmmmmmmm!"

Mine, mine, mine. Everything is either mine, or it's yours. What a blended family needs as soon as possible is something that is *ours*. In this chapter, I'll share some ideas for creating *our* things. These suggestions may not reduce the yelling and fighting over individual toys and possessions, but they *can* help you build your own unique family identity, reduce some of those possessive urges, and give your blended-family members a sense that *we're all in this together.*

Create New Traditions

Despite what my kids say about them, I recommend that you start building your family's unique identity by holding a family meeting. If my experience holds true for you, your kids will think (at least at first) that family meetings are kind of interesting. (OK, so don't expect to actually hear them *say* this, but at least they'll probably show up without being forced or bribed.) Tell them you're starting a new tradition of holding family meetings when everyone needs to know what's going on or when someone needs to share information with everyone in the family. In a family meeting, you want everyone's input, so try to encourage each family member to speak. (This is not a problem in my family. The trouble is getting them to shut up so *I* can speak.)

> *If my experience holds true for you, your kids will think (at least at first) that family meetings are kind of interesting.*

Maybe the first family meeting can be about something fun: drawing names for the family's Christmas gift exchange or sharing ideas about what would be fun for everyone to do on a weekend or summer trip. You could also schedule a low-key family pep rally: gather everyone into a room or around a table, as we did when I was soliciting ideas and information for this book, and just ask everyone to say something nice about each person. If your experience is like ours, there will be a lot of joking and wise cracks but also some wonderfully affirming and encouraging statements of love, admiration, and praise.

In one of our first family meetings as a blended family, we discussed ground rules for borrowing each other's clothes and toys. Another time we asked everyone for ideas about what to do for my parents to surprise them on their anniversary. Kids can be very creative!

Holiday traditions are especially important. Consider calling a family meeting to discover the traditions your two families enjoyed (or didn't) before the blending, then try to reach a compromise about which ones you will and won't observe in your new family. Most important, though, create some holiday traditions that are new to all of you: find a new place to visit on a holiday outing, decide to have more than one Christmas tree and vote for different themes, or make it a regular event to drive around town and look at Christmas lights together.

Or establish a new Christmas Eve or Christmas morning ritual. Maybe you'll be like the family that prolongs the gift opening as long as possible, having the kids serve as elves who deliver gifts to family members one at a time and letting everyone ooh and ah as each gift is opened. Another family has an exuberant all-at-once gift-opening extravaganza, then the family members go around the room with each one telling about his or her gifts with the enthusiasm of Vanna White on *Wheel of Fortune* describing the grand prizes of the day.

Maybe you'll decide to leave something unique for Santa to munch on during his visit: not just milk and cookies but a bowl of popcorn and a soft drink, or a ham sandwich and some eggnog—or even sugar cubes for the reindeer. I heard of one family that bakes a special "birthday cake for Jesus" on Christmas Eve and leaves a slice for Santa to find.

If some of the kids are going to be with their other parent

for the holiday, talk about ways you can share pre-Christmas celebrations. At our house, we find a day when everyone's going to be together, even if it's a week before the actual holiday, and we pretend the holiday is on that day. So, for example, sometime during the week before Thanksgiving, if some or all of our kids are scheduled to be with their other parent on the holiday, I cook a big turkey and drag out the good china, and we simply pretend it's Thanksgiving. On that day I leave out a basket and some slips of paper, and throughout the day family members come by and write down different things they're thankful for. Then, while we've gathered around the table for the meal, we pass the basket around, pull out a slip, and read what it says. Sometimes we know who wrote it. Sometimes we don't. The guessing adds to the fun, and the wide range of things we're thankful for includes ridiculous remarks that make us laugh and poignant things that put a lump in our throats.

Blended families need to establish their own everyday traditions and activities as well. Since we are a musical bunch comprised of kids and adults who know what it's like to be in the spotlight, we've encouraged our kids to "put on shows" for us. I remember one particular Mother's Day when our kids settled Don and me into our easy chairs, pushed back the other furniture in the living room, and put on a musical extravaganza of songs and dance routines that blew us away. There have been smaller, impromptu productions as well, when the kids have called us in to watch "a show we want to do for you." They are especially famous for their Whitney Houston parties, when they lip-synched all Whitney's greatest hits with exaggerated motions and hilarious dance moves.

> *Blended families need to establish their own*
> *everyday traditions and activities as well.*

Our kids also loved to invite their friends over for "dance parties." When they wanted to demonstrate their sock-hop talents, we moved the furniture out of a big room with a hardwood floor and cranked up the stereo so they could dance their hearts out. (Unknown to them, I had sprayed the soles of their socks with Pledge, so while they went through their wild-and-crazy dance moves, Don and I cheered and applauded—and also got the floor polished!)

These living-room concerts and performances weren't typical traditions because they weren't done on the same day every year; they simply occurred whenever the mood struck. Still, they were something our kids could talk about to their friends and say, "Our family does this." So be creative. Think of new activities, celebrations, or commemorations that could give your kids something to tell their friends about, letting them say, "*In our family* we do this thing where we all get together and . . ."

Share Yourselves

One of the best traditions to start is one that lets you help someone else or do something nice for a neighbor. Maybe as a family you could stir up some baked goods and deliver little May baskets full of treats to surprise your neighbors on the first day of May. I heard of one military family who went to the cemetery where relatives were buried and put little flags on the graves of all the veterans. And there's another couple who take their kids with them as they deliver Meals on Wheels one day a week. If your children are old enough, perhaps you could volunteer as a family working on Saturdays to help build a home with Habitat for Humanity. Or you could take one weekend day a month to visit nursing home residents together.

When Jesus said, "'It is more blessed to give than to receive" (Acts 20:35), He knew what He was talking about! When you as a family can do something to help another person, or another family, you get a triple-whammy blessing: you do a good deed that boomerangs back and blesses you, and at the same time you're creating a unique tradition and a shared memory that your family can claim as something that's not just yours, not just mine, but *ours.*

I've seen how my own kids blossom when we reach out together to help others. One simple way this occurs is when they come along on the road with me and help me in my work for World Vision, a charity organization that matches children in need throughout the world with good-hearted sponsors who make monthly donations to provide their "adopted" child with food, clothing, and shelter. During a concert, when I start talking about World Vision, my children climb up on the stage with me, bringing along photographs of youngsters who need sponsors. Then, during the break, they visit with the audience members who come forward, encouraging them to consider sponsoring one of "their" children.

Our House, Our School, Our Church, Our Dog

When Don and I got married, he and his kids moved into the house where my children and I were living. It was a big house that could accommodate our big blended family. But there were two problems with it: it was old, and it wasn't *ours*. The house was grand and historic, but something was always causing problems: the roof, the plumbing, the furnace, the floor, you name it. Because it wasn't well insulated, it was also very expensive to heat and cool. And it sat on a huge lot that cost a fortune to keep mowed and trimmed during the summer.

Also, while I've already described our apparently misguided attempts to make the actual move-in and blending go smoothly, it was obvious that the Peslis kids were constantly aware that they were living in someone else's home.

So we decided to move.

Now, I'm well aware that this isn't an option for all blended families. Often the husband and wife have endured serious financial hits as they've gone through divorce and as they've established a separate home for themselves and their kids. They may be paying alimony, child support, lawyer fees, and other expenses that prevent them from even thinking about moving to a different home. But if it is an option for you, I strongly urge you to consider it. Scout out some possibilities, then bring the kids along to look at the prospective houses so they can have some input.

When Don and I decided we needed to move, it took us a long time to find the house we thought would work for us. We toured the area with agents, looking at possibilities, but the home we eventually settled on was one I happened to drive by one day. I spotted a For Sale sign in the yard, and Don and I checked it out, and we both liked it. Then we packed up the kids and let them do their own inspection. We all agreed this was the house for us, and this time we did plenty of walk-throughs discussing who would have which room. The kids were around and watching when the movers came to pack and move us, so they felt like they were a part of the process. At the new house, they helped unpack and set up their toys and games in their bedrooms, which helped them feel like they were each establishing their own new territory, not moving onto someone else's turf—or having to move their things around to accomodate a newcomer.

When Don and I married, our kids didn't have to change schools, and they were able to continue attending the same schools when we moved into the new house, so everyone was pleased about that. But let me just point out that if you move into a new house and all the kids do have to change schools, especially if they're all going to be attending the same school, that can be another bonding experience.

> *If you move into a new house and all the kids do have to change schools, especially if they're all going to be attending the same school, that can be another bonding experience.*

If you and your kids were happy with their old school, I understand that having to change may be difficult and that this move has the potential to add more sorrow to what the kids may already be feeling about the breakup of their original family. But it's possible that moving into a new house that "belongs" equally to all of you may have some benefits that outweigh the issues of changing schools. And as they head off to that new school, all the kids will be sharing a new experience that creates similar feelings they can discuss later. Ideally, they will encourage each other on that "scary" first day, and after it's over maybe a family meeting can facilitate an exchange of first-day storytelling. In other words, even in the trying and challenging experience of moving to a new school, help your children find the joy!

The same issues apply to the church your family attends. If you're all happily attending the same church when the blending occurs, that's the perfect situation. But if, for one reason or another, you need to find a new church, I urge you to use that as another family-bonding adventure as you go about visiting and considering different congregations until you find one that all (or at least most of you) agree would be a good "ours." Again, just going through that experience can help pull you together as a family as you all settle onto a pew in the various churches you're visiting and feel that "everyone's staring at us." And comparing notes after the service, letting the kids describe the Sunday school classes beginning with a one-to-ten rating scale and then elaborating on their evaluation, can also be an interesting topic for a family meeting or a Sunday lunch.

Of course, I hope you'll find a church that has a vibrant, fun, appealing, inspiring youth group. Keep looking until you find one your kids *want* to be part of. It can make a tremendous difference in the way your children handle life in a blended family.

Here's another idea: bring a new pet into your blended family. Take the kids to the local animal shelter and find a dog or cat they can share as owners. (Of course, no matter what promises you hear, we all know who's *really* going to be feeding that new member of the family, handling housebreaking, cleaning the litter box, and chauffeuring Fido or Fluffy to the vet's office for shots, but still, it can be worth the hassle.)

My kids and I adopted a feisty little mutt named Brownie during our "just us" phase after watching the movie *Homeward Bound.* When our family blended with Don's, Brownie was obviously loyal to us while merely tolerating the newcomers to our household. But then, as a family, we adopted Lucky, a long-bodied, short-legged, big-hearted lover who appears to be a mix between a dachshund and a German shepherd. Sam is the one who first bonded with Lucky as a puppy and convinced us we needed another dog, and I think all the Ganisilapivys (with the possible exception of Brownie) have enjoyed having him grow up with us. Although Sam claims Lucky as his pride and joy, this is a dog who doesn't play favorites. He obviously loves belonging to this whole big, busy family.

And let me just say that yes, there *are* challenges with having two dogs living in the house. For a while there I stopped thinking of my living room carpet as white and instead started saying it had a pastel floral pattern. But then I discovered the most wonderful thing: Invisible Fencing *inside* the house! The installers set up "fences" across the doors to the rooms I decided were off-limits to the dogs, and they wear collars with transmitters that give them a little "charge" if they venture too close. (Now if I could just stop Lucky from chewing on Brownie's transmitter and dragging him around the house by it!)

The Ultimate "Ours"

Whatever activities you repeatedly enjoy together as a blended family can bring you closer together and help establish your identity as a new, separate entity. And whatever you can decide as a family to bring into your home can become additional glue that gives your family a shared sense of ownership and history.

The ultimate "ours" is . . . well, it's a baby.

And not just any baby, but an adopted baby.

OK, I know this is pretty radical. I mean, you may have been rolling your eyes up there in the previous paragraphs when I suggested you adopt a pet. Now I'm telling you to adopt a *baby*?

Well, no. Not all of you. Adoption is a serious matter, a lifelong commitment, and not everyone is cut out to be an adoptive parent. And certainly a lot of couples in second marriages will want to create their own baby to celebrate their new life together. I understand that. Don and I went through those discussions too, just as you may be doing now. But we had already brought *seven* children into the world in our first marriages, and really, that seemed like enough.

Still, the idea would sometimes come up. Then we would look around at the rambunctious family we lived with and slap ourselves back to reality. Then there were those other conversations . . .

Don was an adopted child who had grown up in a loving and supportive home. Both of his adoptive parents had died by the time we married, but whenever they were mentioned, Don might say how good it would be if someday . . . sure, it was crazy . . . but wouldn't it be wonderful if *we* could adopt a child, sort of as a way of passing on the blessing he had been given? "And if it was a boy," Don would say, "maybe we could name him Sam, after my dad."

We are people who believe that abortion is wrong, but we also recognize that if you're going to stand against abortion, you have to stand *for* those children who are born in situations where their parents can't care for them. So to us, especially with Don's background, adoption is something Christians should seriously consider when circumstances allow.

And there was another thing about adopting a child that appealed to us: he or she would belong equally to *all* of us. This wouldn't be anyone's half sister or half brother. He or she would be completely different from any of us. An adopted baby would be the ultimate "ours."

These discussions would occur . . . but nothing would be done about them. We had a full, rewarding life already. We were living happily as a family of nine, and undoubtedly we could have gone on like that forever, except for that one Saturday morning phone call. It was from one of my best friends, Shari Schrock, whose husband, Wes, is an attorney who sometimes handles private adoptions.

"Sandi, I don't even know why I'm calling you," she began. "But this baby has been born. Wes is handling the adoption, and the people who were going to adopt this baby—well, the adoption has fallen through."

Shari wasn't calling to ask if Don and I wanted to adopt this baby. She knew better than to ask a couple who already had seven children if they wanted another one! Instead, she was calling to ask if we knew anyone else who might be thinking of adopting. As Shari explained, "We've called everybody we can think of—the judge, the adoption agencies in this area—and nothing has worked out. Now we're running out of time; if the baby isn't adopted within twenty-four hours, it has to go into the foster-care system. So we're just calling everyone we know to see if anyone knows anybody who is looking to adopt. You don't know anyone, do you?"

To make a long (and wonderful) story short, twenty-four hours later Don and I were standing in a hospital lobby waiting to see this little baby, a multi-racial boy who needed a family. Shari and Wes went to the nursery to bring the baby to us. It may sound rather callous, but honestly, we were just there to *see* him, not necessarily to *adopt* him. We thought—or rather, we hoped—God would somehow give us a sign when we saw the baby that would guide us in knowing what we should do.

And then there he was, bundled in the tiny plastic crib: a beautiful, tawny-skinned, fuzzy-headed little bundle snoozing soundly as though he were perfectly at peace, not knowing or caring that his future was about to be decided. The mere sight of him took our breath away. But then we saw the little heart-shaped name tag stuck to the crib. The nurses had named him when he was born, Shari explained as she wiped away tears and struggled to talk. Shari knew the story of Don's adoptive father. And unlike us, she had already read the name on the tag. We bent down to make out the writing and gasped when we saw what it said.

The mere sight of him took our breath away.

The nurses had named him Sam.

After Shari's call on Saturday, we had held a family meeting to talk with the kids about the possibility of adopting. If anyone, especially one of the older kids, had been adamantly opposed to it, I'm not sure what we would have done. Instead, we were amazed to learn that all the kids loved the idea. Jonathan and Donnie even said they would share their room with their new baby brother. The girls talked about how wonderful it would be to have "our own baby."

On Sunday, after signing papers at the hospital, we came back home and told them what we had done, and everyone let out a whoop.

The attitude was, *we* are adopting a baby!

The announcement launched a whirlwind of activity as we prepared to welcome our new family member. The whole family headed out to Target, where we filled multiple shopping carts with furniture, bedding, diapers, bottles, and practically everything else the store was selling in its newborn department. Then we joyfully headed home for the unpacking, assembling, planning, and laughing.

We—all nine of us—were adopting a baby!

Today Sam loves to hear the story of his adoption, and he loves his family as much as we love him. He is nobody's stepbrother, nobody's half brother. For all of our children, he is, without question, *their* brother, shared and loved equally. Perhaps more than anything, Sam has been the strongest glue melding our blended family into one cohesive unit.

If you're considering adding another member to your blended family, I hope you'll consider adopting. There's a Sam (or a Samantha) out there who needs a family, and he or she might be just what your family needs too.

And if you can't adopt a child to become part of your family and live in your home, consider sponsoring a World Vision child. For a small monthly gift, you can become involved in the life of a needy youngster half a world away. The exchange of letters and photos can be a rewarding and educational experience for you and your family to share as you watch that child grow and thrive thanks to your help.

We've also opened our home as an unofficial way station for children who've ended up in difficult situations due to family problems and breakups. These temporary family members, usually referred to us by our church or through friends, have been another means for us to work *together* to help someone else. Usually this child's arrival means that one of our kids has agreed to share or give up his or her room temporarily so that the new arrival has a comfortable and safe place to sleep and stow belongings. We also work together to make sure this guest feels welcomed and loved.

By sharing ourselves with others, we all receive the benefits of knowing we're faithfully following Jesus's directives to "love each other as I have loved you" (John 15:12) and "do to others as you would have them do to you" (Luke 6:31). What better traditions can there be for any family to establish?

Another Adoption

Two years ago, through a remarkable set of events, Don was able to identify his birth parents. For the kids and me, watching from the sidelines, the experience unfolded like an exciting novel as one by one the pieces of the puzzle fell into place. Sadly, the first bit of news revealed that Don's birth mother had died, but he was thrilled to connect with her sister (his aunt) and other members of his maternal family. Then we set to work looking for his birth father. When it looked like he had been found, there were DNA tests, and finally the phone call came, bringing with it those amazing words, "Hello, Don. This is your dad."

> *Finally the phone call came, bringing with it those amazing words, "Hello, Don. This is your dad."*

Since that moment, our whole family has adopted another newcomer into our fold. His name is Jim Perry, but we call him Pop. By blood, he is the father of Don and the grandfather of Donnie, Aly, and Mollie. But to our way of thinking, he was discovered after our family blended; therefore, he belongs to all of us.

And that seems fine with him. In fact, as I'm writing this book, he is living with us as he recovers from open-heart surgery, and we are all thrilled to have him here. In the last two years, he has tried his best to make up for the forty-some years of Don's life that he missed before the two found each other, and we've all enjoyed watching to see what creative surprise he comes up with next.

One example came at Christmastime, when we all flew to Miami on December 26, 2004. It would be Don's first time to celebrate the holiday with his newly discovered birth family, which includes not only his father but *four* fabulous brothers—Jim, John, Richie, and Lenny—and their families. Suddenly Don went from being an only child to being one of five siblings! It was a wild and laughter-filled visit as we all got acquainted with the members of our newly expanded family. Technically, these fun-loving people are related only to Don's side of our blended family, but don't try to tell that to Anna, Jenn, Jon, Erin, Sam, or me. Like Don, Donnie, Aly, and Mollie, we truly consider them *ours.*

And here's the clever surprise Pop had waiting for Don that year: a Christmas stocking embroidered with "Baby's First Christmas"!

I mentioned earlier that Don had started referring to Donnie sometimes as "Number One" after a "wonderful thing" happened in our family. Well, now you know what that wonderful thing was. Don is the oldest of Jim Perry's five sons, and one day, out of the blue, Pop started calling Don "Number One." It's just a little thing, really. But it has meant so much to Don; it's made him feel wonderful. After all these years of being an only child, of not knowing anything about his birth family, to suddenly discover that family and then to be treated respectfully by his father as a firstborn son, well, you have to admit, that's pretty wonderful.

Having Pop in our family has added a rich new dimension to our blended family, not the least of which is the fact that now, when someone calls out on the intercom, "I have to be at youth group in twenty minutes!" I often hear Pop's friendly voice in reply, saying, "I'll be glad to take you."

The Gift of Grandparents

Now that we have found Don's dad, and since he spends a big part of the year with us, we're fortunate to have a loving grandparent in our home helping us tend the flock. He's always quick to help anytime we need him.

Before we found each other, Pop had only sons and grandsons; now he also has five granddaughters, and it's been interesting to see how he has creatively adapted his grandparenting style to embrace *all* his grandkids, including the girls.

Pop isn't the only grandparent who's become one of *ours.* Through the years our kids have been blessed by a host of loving grandparents, including the Peslis kids' maternal grandparents and my own kids' paternal grandparents. In my experience, there can be something godly and powerful about a strong, supportive relationship between grandparents and grandchildren, whether they're related by blood or marriage. I've seen that relationship transcend family lines and ooze over hard feelings, helping youngsters who feel like they're stuck in the chop and mix cycles feel loved by an even wider circle of people.

The kids' Helvering grandparents are now in heaven, but

while they were alive they adored the kids and played an important role in helping us raise them. Now that they're gone, and with the Peslis kids' maternal grandparents living far away, Pop and my parents, Ron and Carolyn Patty, are the grandparents who are most involved in our children's everyday lives.

> *Like Pop, they have infused our family with love and laughter in a way no one outside the family could do.*

From the first day it became apparent that my family would be blending with Don's, Mom and Dad have considered Donnie, Aly, and Mollie, and later, Sam, as much their grandchildren as they do Anna, Jenn, Jon, and Erin. They are "Nana" and "Papa" to the whole tribe, and grandparents everywhere could take lessons from them on how to show a blended family unconditional love and enduring support. They live just a few blocks away and are always out there in the audience, cheering on all the kids' show-choir performances, sitting in the stands at Sam's ball games, willing to help with homework, or ready to fix a lunch. They are ache-soothers, storytellers, comfort-givers, rapt listeners, and unflagging supporters. They are there for us when we need them. Like Pop, they are quick to volunteer their chauffeuring service, and also like Pop, they have infused our family with love and laughter in a way no one outside the family could do. What blessings these loved ones have been to us!

* * *

Whether it's by claiming grandparents, adopting a pet (or a child or an in-law), making a household move, developing new traditions, or through some other way, a blended family needs to write its own unique history, establishing its identity as something different from its component parts. Make it an adventure! Go out there and find yourselves.

8.

Head Lice and Bedbugs

*Coping with a Family That's Bigger
Than It Was Before*

You've given me a staggering task, ruling this mob of
people. Yes, give me wisdom and knowledge as I come
and go among this people—for who on his own is
capable of leading these, your glorious people?
—2 Chronicles 1:9–10 MSG

I can empathize with King Solomon as he looked out over
his "mob of people" and considered the "staggering task"
he'd been given. When you're a parent in a second marriage,
you're probably overseeing a family that is bigger than it was
before, and sometimes that task can seem absolutely over-
whelming. For me, those are the times when I'm feeling
futile and frustrated, and a magnet on my refrigerator
becomes my mothering motto. It says, "Some days I feel like

all I'm doing is rearranging the deck chairs onboard the *Titanic*."

One of those frustrating—and funny—times came last year when both Jonathan and Sam were sick and had to stay home several days from school . . . all day . . . every day . . . together . . . getting on each other's nerves . . . and mine. On weekday mornings, I usually get up at 5:45 so I can throw some breakfast together before the "mob" comes running down the stairs, blows through the kitchen, and zips out the door on the way to school. Then, after everyone's been delivered to wherever they're supposed to be, and when frantic phone calls have been answered and forgotten items have been hurriedly rushed to the anxious one waiting on the sidewalk in front of the school, I get to enjoy a few hours of peace and quiet.

This is *my time*. However, when the kids are sick and have to stay home from school, I'm happy to share "my time" and settle in for some cozy talk time or maybe curl up with the droopy one and watch a movie or nap together on the couches. But there was nothing cozy or cuddly about Jonathan and Sam's last sick day at home. I knew they were better when their bickering and yelling and fighting changed from infrequent outbursts to battles that raged hour after hour.

Finally I'd had enough. "You guys are driving me crazy!" I said.

Then I gave myself a time out in my room.

Pretty soon there was a knock at my door. The two boys sheepishly peeked in and said, "Mom, we're sorry." Then Jonathan added, "We weren't really fighting. We were *bonding*."

Oh, brother! Any more "bonding," and I think I would have been bound over to the funny farm.

Parenting a family that's bigger than it was before can be exhausting. I read somewhere that at least one state government mandates that group homes can have no more than eight children, and the house parents in that group home can't have outside employment—because parenting eight kids is considered a full-time job.

An even more surprising statistic is one I heard on *Oprah*: an interviewed expert said raising two children and being a stay-at-home mom is equivalent to *three* full-time jobs. So, if you do the math, that gives me the equivalent of twelve full-time jobs, plus a full-time music career, which puts me right over the weight limit for exhaustion.

In bigger families, we parents don't get a lot of "my time" when we can relax and recoup our strength for the next go-round. Someone's always intruding into those precious moments with a runny nose, a forgotten backpack, or a need to talk. But there's a lot of fun to be had in these newly expanded families, even in our exhaustion. To find it, we need to ask God for "wisdom and knowledge," as King Solomon did, and we need to keep a positive perspective.

Choose to See the Good

My home is a crazy place, but I love being here. My big, blended family is exhausting, but it's exhilarating too. Somehow I actually seem to thrive on this strange, Ganisilapivy-style chaos. Actually, it doesn't happen "somehow." It happens because I've chosen to find the joy in the midst of mayhem.

Truth be told, sometimes it's hard to find anything in this house.

Truth be told, sometimes it's hard to find *anything* in this house. Right now, eleven of us are calling it home: Don and me, seven of the eight kids (Mollie is in Michigan), plus Pop and a long-term teenage houseguest who needed a place of refuge. Count in Brownie and Lucky, Charly the cat, and the assorted hamsters, lizards, and other critters Sam has collected, and we've pretty much got a houseful! And our house isn't just full of people; it's full of *stuff*. Last year when I was helping Anna pack up so she could move into her own home (actually a house she's sharing with some other college students), I called Don excitedly and told him, "What do you know? There *is* carpet in Anna's room after all!"

I joke that my next book will be titled, *I Long for a House without Clutter: One Woman's Personal Pipe Dream.* Let me tell you what I'm talking about.

If you walked into my house right now, the first thing you would see is boxes of books stacked by the front door that I have to take to an upcoming ladies' luncheon I'm doing. If I move them somewhere out of sight, I'll forget to take them. So there they sit for another ten days.

Hanging in the dining room is Aly's beautiful long dress that she wore for her recent solo competition; she doesn't have enough room in her closet (too much stuff!), and we don't want to smash it. So there it hangs, right above my computer bag. I'm heading out on the road again tomorrow, and I have to remember to take it with me.

Laundry is piled on the kitchen counter, waiting to be folded. Beach towels are draped over the barstools; I'm not sure why, since it's still too cold to swim. Sam's baseball uniform is hanging on one of the drawer pulls. He has a game tonight, and I have to take his uniform to Nana's house later; she's picking him up from school and taking him to the game while I take Erin to a dentist appointment. Don and I will rendezvous at the game as soon as we can get there.

Sam's poster-board artwork is leaning up against the wall; I don't know where to put it but can't bear to throw it away. The weekly bulletin from his teacher is posted on the refrigerator, and a permission slip for the prom is lying on the counter. Jonathan's date is coming down from Michigan to go with him, so this form had to be filled out and signed by all the parents and the principal at each high school. We've spilled Diet Coke on it twice and Gatorade once; I just hope the signatures are still readable. And let me just throw in here that this year *five* Ganisilapivys are doing the prom thing! That alone is probably enough to put "normal" moms in the psych ward!

Several pairs of tennis shoes are scattered around the family room. There's a baseball on the coffee table alongside a bag of change one of the kids has collected, hoping we can go to the bank soon and make a deposit. Schoolbooks are stacked beside the couch. In the hallway, clothes that have come back from the dry cleaner are waiting to be carried upstairs.

In addition to all this small stuff, until last week we had Pop's hospital bed in the office with all the necessary medical supplies and equipment. He had *seven* bypasses, and we were glad he agreed to come here so we could all encourage him during his recovery.

The house isn't *dirty*—my dedicated cleaning ladies just made their weekly visit—but it's seriously cluttered.

I could put all the things away, and sometimes I do. But usually, instead of spending my day putting every little thing back in its place, I choose to spend my time tolerating the clutter and feeling thankful that the kids' stuff is here. It's an indication that they're still in my life, living under my roof, and I love having them here.

You see, it's all a matter of perspective. I hope, as you view the clutter of your larger, blended family, you'll choose to find the blessings there too. Then let that attitude spread from your home to the world around you. Here's an example of the way I try to keep a positive perspective:

I'm thankful for the piles of laundry, because it means my loved ones are nearby . . .

For the mess to clean up after a party, because it means I've been surrounded by friends . . .

For the lady who sings really off-key behind me in church, because it means I can hear . . .

For the wrinkles I see when I look in the mirror, because, well, they don't hurt . . .

For the alarm clock that goes off in the wee hours of the morning, because it means I'm alive . . .

For the clothes that sometimes fit a little too snuggly, because it means I have enough to eat (and let me just add that my closet is very organized by size: 14, 16, 18, and "none of your business"!) . . .

For the homework that I have to help with after school, because it means someone needs me . . .

For the problems I've gone through, because they have brought me closer to God . . .

For the disagreements that swirl throughout our country, because they mean we are a *free* people who can speak as we please.

This kind of upbeat attitude actually comes from the Bible. The apostle Paul said, "You'll do best by filling your minds and meditating on things true, noble, reputable, authentic, compelling, gracious—the best, not the worst; the beautiful, not the ugly; things to praise, not things to curse" (Philippians 4:8 MSG). I love that verse, but honestly, I think it has been my kids who have helped me most to fill my mind and meditate on "the beautiful, not the ugly." After all, they're the ones who are constantly reminding me, in their laughter-sprinkled, teasing voices, "Find the joy, Mom! You've gotta find the joy!"

> *I think it has been my kids who have helped me most to fill my mind and meditate on "the beautiful, not the ugly."*

They've even given me one of their own attitude-adjustment items to add to my thankfulness list. They say, "We're thankful to have a curfew (although we always wish it could be later), because it means someone cares about us."

I'm thankful my kids can still teach their mom a thing or two.

Of course there's always at least one jokester in the group ready to make some wisecrack about my positive perspective and grateful attitude. When I was on a long road trip last year, I called home and told Sam I would be so glad to see him, that when I got back I would kiss him all over his face.

He was quiet for a minute and finally said, "Uh, Mom? Are you gonna have lipstick on? Because I don't want that stuff all over me."

Setting the Tone

There's something contagious about a grateful attitude and a positive perspective, especially when they're lived out in the midst of challenges or hardships. Remember that as a parent, you set the tone for your family. It's like when we're gathered as a family, ready to sing a cappella ("I Believe" is our favorite family song to sing together), and we ask Jonathan to find that starting note for us. When he pulls it out of his head and hums it to us, we're off and singing. Honestly, it's a sound so glorious, my eyes tear up, and my nose starts running, and, well, the music is beautiful, but *I* am not a pretty sight! Other times someone else may start us off, and if the key is too high or too low we either have to stop, regroup, and start over, or we stretch our voices until we sound like either screeching parakeets or water pipes booming in the basement.

Your mood can help make your home a happy place, and there's no better way to develop a happy mood than to practice an attitude of gratitude everywhere you go (and, OK, for those moms at a certain age, sometimes hormone therapy helps too). I've seen that lesson played out in so many ways, but particularly during a couple of recent performances.

Your mood can help make your home a happy place.

During a Women of Faith conference last year, I was delighted to learn that a sweet friend of mine named Lisa would be in the audience. She is a wonderful and unique young lady, a Down's syndrome girl whom others might label "special needs." Lisa has some pretty severe physical problems. And yet, as I have watched her move through life, I've seen her share genuine joy and a positive perspective wherever she goes. Recently she learned sign language, and as she and her mother have attended many of my concerts, I've seen her sign some of my songs. Her beautiful style of expression just knocks me out.

At that Women of Faith conference, I invited Lisa to come up on the stage and sign the words as I sang "Shout to the Lord." So up she ran, and her amazingly joyful spirit absolutely captivated the audience of several thousand women as she interpreted the words of the song in her sweet and elegant way.

Marilyn Meberg said afterward, "We can talk about joy all we want, but watching Lisa, we see it firsthand."

That's the kind of person I want to be for my family. Even when the house is cluttered, the kids are yelling, and chaos reigns—even when I get frustrated and give myself a time out or start banging and clanging things in the kitchen (I'll be the first, second, and third one to tell you that far too many times I mess up, big-time)—even then, I hope my family can see joy lived out "firsthand" in me.

Another incident on stage demonstrated again how powerful the gift of joyful gratitude can be. I was part of a benefit concert in Texarkana, Arkansas, for Watersprings Ranch, a place for kids who need a home. Some of the kids are there for a few months, some for a few years, and for some the ranch becomes their permanent home. It's a good and nurturing and joy-filled place, but probably all of the kids who happily live there would prefer to be in a stable family where Mom and Dad show them lots of love. These kids don't have that, but when I'm with them, I'm amazed by their happy natures and grateful attitudes. At the concert, they sang "The Gift Goes On" with me, and we were awesome, if I do say so myself.

When I was getting ready to sing my last song, "Christmas Was Meant for Children," one of the boys unexpectedly appeared beside me onstage. He looked like he wanted to say something, so I gave him the microphone. He asked if the other kids could come up onstage and give me a hug to say thank you for doing the concert "so we could have clothes and food and stuff."

I started to cry, and so did the people in the audience. I welcomed the other kids back to the stage, and they sat with me while I sang that last song. Then it occurred to me that some of the other kids might want to say something too. They began to raise their hands, and one at a time, they expressed sweet gratitude to those who had attended the concert. They thanked the patrons for helping make their time at Watersprings Ranch so special. They thanked their teachers as well as their house parents and the directors of the ranch. It was such a meaningful time for all of us. I had come to that place to make the evening special for the kids and their guests, but what I did couldn't hold a candle to the gracious attitude those "underprivileged" kids showed all of us that night.

The Fun of Imperfection

I've heard it said that we learn more from our mistakes than from our successes. If that's true, I should be a genius by now! I think there's a corollary to that adage for blended families coping with being bigger than they were before: bigger families have bigger problems and make bigger messes, so we have bigger things to laugh about later (assuming we survive the big messes we make). In fact, sometimes it's the things that go wrong that end up meaning the most to us.

Case in point: our family vacation in Greece. Actually it

was part of a cruise event I hosted annually for a group called Forever Friends. Usually we sailed the Caribbean, but that year I wanted to do something special, so I set up the Forever Friends cruise in the Mediterranean and brought along Don and the kids as my "special talent." (Hey, whatever it takes.)

So, after months and months of planning, we finalized a complicated but thrilling itinerary for the ten of us Ganisilapivys in conjunction with the cruise. We would fly from Indianapolis to Atlanta, then on to London, where we would change airlines and fly to Italy to enjoy a couple of days in Venice before joining our Forever Friends on the cruise ship. We would sail across the Mediterranean to Greece, and then our family would spend some additional days sightseeing and soaking up the wonders of the ancient world.

Ask my kids today about that elaborate trip, and not one of them will mention visiting the Acropolis or the Parthenon. They don't remember a thing about Venice or cruising the Mediterranean either. What they like to talk about is, first, how we got stuck in the Atlanta airport for *two days*. We landed there just as a huge storm swept up the East Coast, closing the airport. The storm finally ended, but all the flights to London were full, for the next two days. Well, maybe not full, but they didn't have ten empty seats, which is what we needed. So there we sat (and slept) on the floor of the airport for forty-eight hours.

The kids loved it. We played endless card games, we ate

every kind of airport junk food available, we exercised by parading up and down the long concourse, and best of all, we talked and talked and talked.

Then came the next adventure: changing planes in London. Our connection was a little tight, and when we stopped at the desk and asked, the gate agent said pleasantly, "Your flight will be leaving from gate ninety." I can't remember what gate we'd come in at, but we all remember that it was a *long* way to gate ninety. We loaded up the mountain of luggage onto several baggage carts, put the smallest kids in the seats, and set off at a trot for the other end of the airport. But when we got there . . . it wasn't our flight! We realize *now* that the pleasant gate agent was saying, in her crisp British accent, "Your flight will be leaving from gate NINE-teen."

Now we were really late, so we made a quick U-turn and raced back up the concourse. Can you picture this galloping, ten-member assemblage of parents, kids, luggage, and carts frantically speeding through the airport? Can you do it without laughing? Not us!

But that wasn't the last adventure (and you'll notice there's still nothing about the Parthenon). We landed in Venice and rushed off to the cruise ship (forget sightseeing; we had used up our two buffer days in Atlanta), arriving less than two hours before it departed. Then we sailed on over to Greece to do the sightseeing thing.

One afternoon in between tours, we found ourselves with

a little free time, and we rounded up the kids, waved down two taxis, and asked the lead driver to take us to a *family* beach. The taxis dropped us off, Don paid the fare, then we made the short walk down to the beach. And yes, indeed, it was a *family* beach, full of parents and youngsters, teenagers, middle-aged sunbathers, and old people, all frolicking in the surf, jogging over the sand, even playing badminton and volleyball—*most of them topless if not totally nude!*

We hurried our little covey of big-eyed children down to the water, urging them to watch where they stepped (hoping they would keep their eyes on their feet instead of the naked people around us). Some of the kids handled the situation better than others, but Jonathan, in particular, was mortified by where we'd taken him. "Mom, we can't stay here!" he said.

"Honey, let's just make the best of it. Go on with the others and play in the water a little while; just ignore those other people. You're from Indiana! Go enjoy the ocean! Have fun and don't think about anything else," I told him.

Reluctantly, Jon headed down to the water to join Don and the rest of the family. He splashed around in the surf for a while, but then a big wave rolled in unexpectedly and smacked him right in the face. He turned and ran headlong up the beach, his eyes full of salt water, and tumbled right into a topless, middle-aged, female jogger, his face landing right in her chest. Poor Jonathan was so mortified, when he finally got back to our pile of stuff, he curled up in a little ball, covered his head completely with a beach towel, and refused to open his eyes until we left. The rest of the kids came up later and said, "What's wrong with Jonathan?"

"Don't ask," I told them.

That trip full of missed planes and misadventures is just one instance of how we have come to appreciate (later) the things that go wrong even more than we do the things that go right.

The Head Lice Ordeal

And then there was the year we had head lice.

Now, just let me say, before I tell you this story, that even before our families blended, as a mother of four children, I was quite experienced in the principles of infectious and contagious ailments. After all, I had lived through the ordeal of having a child (eight-year-old Anna) break out with chicken pox in between the first and second halves of a dance recital, probably infecting the whole cast and most of the audience! (But really, I couldn't be concerned about all of them; I soon had my hands full with my own little isolation ward and four little chicken-poxed patients.)

I'm also the mother who, after we had blended, would not hesitate in a physician's office to ask, when a child was diagnosed with strep throat, "Uh, Doctor, would you mind just writing out seven more prescriptions of the antibiotic to save me the extra trips?"

Head Lice and Bedbugs

I had weathered all sorts of contagious viruses and infections, and I felt confident I could handle anything else that tried to attack my family. But then the head lice sneaked in. Looking back on it now, Don and I laugh hysterically. But when it happened, we were just plain hysterical.

> *Looking back on it now, Don and I laugh hysterically.*
> *But when it happened, we were just plain hysterical.*

Let me point out that we were experienced, even in head lice. When the kids were little, we'd had a brief encounter with one or two of the kids. We'd done the treatment, and the lice had disappeared.

Then came the year when the upper grades at the kids' elementary school had a short exchange program with a school overseas, and one of the exchange students stayed briefly with us. Jenn was especially excited about having a friend from overseas, and she offered to share her room with this pleasant young guest student—I'll call her Francine.

All went well for a while, then one morning Jenn came in and whispered, "Mom, Francine's got head lice!"

"How do you know?" I whispered back.

"I just know, Mom! I'm sure of it," Jenn said.

When Francine came down for breakfast, I took a quick, discreet look, standing over her briefly while she ate her cereal. What I saw made me want to scream. Her hair was *full* of lice; they were everywhere.

"Oh, honey, it looks like you've got something in your hair," I said, trying to stay calm. "You know, I think it might be . . . well, it looks like you might have a thing we call head lice. Don't worry. It's no big deal. We'll take care of it. You'll be fine."

I rushed to the store and bought a box of RID then used the kit's fine-tooth comb to get the hundreds, or more accurately, thousands—maybe even *millions*—of nits out of Francine's very, very thick, shoulder-length black hair. It was such an ordeal, I silently prayed as I worked that I wouldn't have to do this job more than once.

Little did I know!

I called the exchange students' adviser at school to alert her to the possibility that the other exchange students— and their host families—might have lice as well. *Then* it occurred to me that I should check the rest of our kids too. That's when the real nightmare began.

We all had head lice. Even Sam, who was still a baby. And even Don and I had them!

We *all* had head lice. Even Sam, who was still a baby. And even Don and I had them!

(Can you imagine what it was like for me during this ordeal to perform in concert, standing up there on stage with my fancy show clothes and makeup on, thinking, *I hope no one finds out I have head lice?*)

An unbelievably intense ritual soon began: Every day for a week or so, as soon as the kids came home from school, I would wash their hair in the sink, comb it out, then use the little fine-tooth comb to pull out any nits. Next I would spray their hair with Lysol (yes, Lysol), put a plastic bag over their hair, wrap their head in a towel, and park them in front of the television for two hours.

Don and I treated each other and finally managed to conquer our lice. But for the kids, the misery was just beginning.

These were the days when the red bag had to go back and forth between the kids' dad's house and our house. I told their dad about the lice and sent along the RID kits, but despite everyone's best efforts, we just could not get those lice to die. They would seem to go away, then I'd do a random check and find that they had reappeared.

School ended, Francine went home, summer began, and the head lice continued.

One of the problems (I know now) is that I was doing the "hair thing" very thoroughly, but I wasn't following the rest of the instructions on the RID bottle and other guidelines I found online. Finally I wised up and performed the full, exhausting ritual. In addition to the hair washing, spraying, bagging, and combing, every morning when the kids got up, I also stripped their beds, put the sheets and pillowcases in a plastic bag and sprayed them thoroughly with Lysol, tied the bag, and put it in the basement where it would stay three weeks to let the death-spray work. Then I sprayed their mattresses and the carpet around their beds.

One week I went room by room, taking everything out of every drawer and giving it the same treatment as the bedding. To this day whenever I smell Lysol or bleach, I think, *Head lice.*

We finally got the boys' infestation under control by cutting off all their hair. But for the girls, especially Aly and Jenn with their long, silky tresses, the head lice lived on.

You're only supposed to use RID every two weeks, as I recall. Soon, like a possessed madwoman, I started using it every day. I started checking the kids before they came into the house, washing the infected kids' hair outside with the garden hose, and combing out the nits before they came inside. Then I would bring them into the mudroom and make them take off all their clothes and put on new ones.

We cleaned out backpacks. We didn't wear hats or ball caps. We sprayed *everything* with Lysol, washed *everything* in bleach, and easily could have used a tanker-truckload of RID. We did so much laundry, I'm sure our water bill doubled. Finally, after what seemed like *years* of agony, we got rid of the head lice. Thank You, Jesus! The head lice went away just as my mind was starting to disappear as well.

Now, just let me take a moment here to point out a lesson I learned from the head-lice calamity. It's a perfect example of how we learn from our mistakes, and it applies to life as well as lice. You don't want to admit you have head lice, just as you probably don't want to admit you have sin in your life. Once that sin is identified, however, and you decide to get serious about cleaning up your act—decide that you're really going to get rid of the junk in your life, such as addiction, a toxic relationship, or whatever it may be, then you have to do a *thorough* cleansing. You can't do it halfway, as I did when I was treating the kids' hair but not their clothes and bedding.

You have to read the directions. For Christians, those directions are found in the Bible. Read it, study it, and learn from it. For moms treating their kids' head lice, the directions are on the bottle of RID and on the Internet. I read part of the directions, but I didn't read them all. As a result, my family spent a lot more time in head-lice land than we should have.

Get Help

Another important thing I've learned from all these misadventures in our big, blended family is that I should ask for help when I need it. Don't be afraid to inquire at your kids' school or in your church or around your neighborhood about parenting support groups, baby-sitting co-ops, mothers'-day-out programs, and any other available support service. Your church's youth group may have teenagers who are interested in making a little extra money by baby-sitting or running errands for you. Many churches offer a program called the Stephen's Ministry, which assists individuals or families in need.

Ask around to find parents who are going through what you're dealing with and find out how they're handling those issues.

Seek out other parents who are willing to carpool with you to get the kids to school or after-school activities. Ask around to find parents who are going through what you're dealing with and find out how they're handling those issues. When I finally felt brave enough to admit to another school mom that my kids had head lice, she said, "Oh, that's such a pain. My kids had head lice last year, and I thought I'd never get rid of them."

Hellllooooooo! Earth to Sandi: why didn't you speak up sooner? This mom could have told you what finally worked for her and saved you at least two months of hair-rific torment.

And don't just ask for help with your kids. Find the help you need for yourself too. If you can afford a house-cleaning service, don't feel one moment of guilt for signing up for it. I predict you'll come to believe it's worth every cent.

If you feel the need for emotional therapy, ask your pastor to recommend a Christian counselor. My kids may have thought it was a waste of time, but I can assure you that it wasn't. I've benefited tremendously myself through my own work with skilled and caring therapists. A good mental-health professional begins by listening and validating your feelings, whatever they are, then helps you bring into the sunlight the reasons why those feelings are troubling you and eventually helps you resolve the problematic issues.

Look around. Ask questions. And *pray*. My experience has been that God will provide for us exactly what we need, whether it's something big, like a happily blended family, or something small, like a gentle hug.

Troubles happen. Hearts break. But God is steadfast. In difficult times, when big-family problems challenge you, "draw close to God, and God will draw close to you" (James 4:8 NLT).

When Don and I were in Hawaii for a performance at Pearl Harbor on the Fourth of July, we called home to talk to Sam (the other kids were with their other parents). My mom was staying at our house with him, and she told Don that the night before, Sam had gone to our closet, pulled out one of Don's T-shirts, and put it on. He told Nana he "just had to be close to Daddy."

It was all Don could do to keep from rushing off to the airport and catching the next flight home! He loves his children passionately, and he always wants to stay close to them.

God feels the same way about us; He likes having us "draw close."

Moving Up from the Back Row

Maybe you've been through some difficult times on your way to becoming a happily blended family. That's certainly my history. Maybe you're having a hard time finding the joy in the hectic struggles of a family that may have doubled in size while you're also coping with headaches like custody issues, visitation rights, and how to be a successful stepparent. I know all about those struggles. I also know it's easy to let bitterness creep in and broken parts stay broken. It takes work to overcome those feelings, and that work begins when you ask God for help.

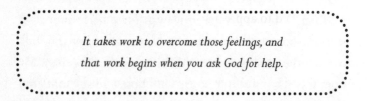

*It takes work to overcome those feelings, and
that work begins when you ask God for help.*

In any kind of blended family, there are always situations or circumstances that can hurt us and wound us deeply. Some are self-imposed, but many are brought upon us by others' woundedness. When we come to Him as victims, He transforms us into victors. I love that!

My journey back to wholeness and happiness started with me crying my heart out on the back row of a church one Sunday morning. But I'm not stuck on that back row anymore. God found me there and, through His grace and goodness, brought me back into the fold. He restored me and gave me a big, fantastic family and a wonderful life more fulfilling than anything I ever could have dreamed of.

It's a dynamic, love-filled, chaos-clad, whirlwind existence, this life in the blender. Some days the blender does a good job of smooth and delicate blending. Some days it's busily chopping and mincing. Then there are those days when everyone feels like they've been turned into puree. For me, living in a happily blended family is pleasant and exciting and fulfilling. But it's more than just day-to-day living. It's a gift from God, a sign of His forgiveness, a symbol of His blessings, and a reminder of His faithfulness.

It's not a perfect life; we're not a perfect family. But we've learned to appreciate our imperfections. I know that, sprinkled among the good times ahead, there will be some hard times too. Try as I might, I know I'm going to make some mistakes, and so will my family. But God has proven Himself trustworthy, and I believe with all my heart that the grace He has lavished on me in the past will be there for me in the future. I know this is true, because I've learned it firsthand. I'm living proof that "the Lord takes broken pieces and by His love makes us whole."

OTHER SELECTIONS FOR WOMEN OF FAITH

Best-Selling authors and Women of Faith® speakers Patsy Clairmont, Mary Graham, Barbara Johnson, Marilyn Meberg, Grammy Award Winning singer Sandi Patty, Luci Swindoll, Sheila Walsh, Thelma Wells and dramatist Nicole Johnson bring humor and insight to women's daily lives. Sit back, exhale, and enjoy spending some time with these extraordinary women!

AVAILABLE WHEREVER BOOKS ARE SOLD.

THOMASNELSON.COM | WOMENOFFAITH.COM

W PUBLISHING GROUP
A Division of Thomas Nelson Publishers
Since 1798
wpublishinggroup.com

NELSON BOOKS
A Division of Thomas Nelson Publishers
Since 1798
thomasnelson.com

WOMEN OF FAITH
womenoffaith.com

COUNTRYMAN
A Division of Thomas Nelson P
Since 1798
thomasnelson.com